Published by

THE BIBLE FOR TODAY PRESS

900 Park Avenue

Collingswood, New Jersey 08108

U.S.A.

Pastor D. A. Waite, Th.D., Ph.D.

𝕭𝖎𝖇𝖑𝖊 𝕱𝖔𝖗 𝕿𝖔𝖉𝖆𝖞 𝕭𝖆𝖕𝖙𝖎𝖘𝖙 𝕮𝖍𝖚𝖗𝖈𝖍

Church Phone: 856-854-4747

BFT Phone: 856-854-4452

Orders: 1-800-John 10:9

e-mail: BFT@BibleForToday.org

Website: www.BibleForToday.org

fax: 856-854-2464

We Use and Defend

The King James Bible

January, 2011

BFT 3482

ISBN #978-1-56848-074-9

𝕬𝖈𝖐𝖓𝖔𝖜𝖑𝖊𝖉𝖌𝖒𝖊𝖓𝖙𝖘

I wish to acknowledge the assistance of the following people:

- **Yvonne Sanborn Waite**--my wife, for encouraging me to publish these questions and answers, for reading the manuscript carefully; and for giving other helpful suggestions for the body of the book and for the cover.

- **Barbara Egan**--our retired **Bible For Today** secretary, for proofreading the manuscript; for suggesting various corrections; and for making valuable comments.

- **Julia Monaghan**--a faithful supporter of our **Bible For Today** ministry and an attender via the Internet of our **Bible For Today Baptist Church** services, who read the manuscript and gave helpful comments for correction.

- **Daniel S. Waite**--the Assistant to the **Bible For Today** Director, who kept my computer working properly; helped with the printing, and made important suggestions.

- **Dr. and Mrs. H. D. Williams**--friends in the **Bible For Today** and the **Dean Burgon Society** ministries, and attenders via the Internet of our **Bible For Today Baptist Church** services whose expertise in "print on demand" (POD) technology has made it possible for us to print this book in this manner, thus saving us hundreds of dollars in costs.

FOREWORD

- **Eight Sections**. This is the third series of 200 questions from the many that have been sent to me through the years (## 401-600). I have answered them as simply and as clearly as possible. The answers to questions ##1-200 can be found in **BFT #3309 @ $12.00 + $7.00 S&H**. The answers to questions ##201-400 can be found in **BFT #3373 @ $12.00 + $7.00 S&H**.

- **The Order Of Questions**. Based on the number of questions in each topic, I have listed questions about the New Testament Greek texts, theological problems, New Testament word meanings, Chinese Union Version, various Bible versions, the King James Bible, and Old Testament word meanings.

- **Miscellaneous Questions**. In this question and answer book, there are eight miscellaneous topics: (1) various books; (2) Bible For Today materials; (3) local church matters; (4) Old Testament Hebrew; (5) prophecy; (6) divorce and remarriage; (7) the Spanish Bible; and (8) the Dean Burgon Society.

- **Various Questions and Answers Are Similar**. I have tried not to duplicate questions and answers in this third book. However, various things should be understood by the readers. Similar questions might have been asked in books one and two. Similar questions might also have been asked in this third book. But if there is a slightly different emphasis either in the question, or in my answer, I have included them. Be sure to consult the very detailed INDEX in this book to help you.

D. a. Waite

Pastor D. A. Waite, Th.D., Ph.D.
Director of the **Bible For Today**, Incorporated, and
Pastor of the **Bible For Today Baptist Church**

Table of Contents

Publisher's Data i

Acknowledgments ii

Foreword iii

Table of Contents iv

Introductory Considerations 1

I. Questions about the New Testament Greek Texts . . 3

II. Questions about Theological Problems 37

III. Questions about New Testament Word Meanings 67

IV. Questions about the Chinese Union Version . . 85

V. Questions about Various Bible Versions 103

VI. Questions about the King James Bible 119

VII. Questions about Old Testament Word Meanings 133

VIII. Questions about Miscellaneous Subjects 145

  1. Various Books 145

  2. Bible For Today Materials 151

  3. Local Church Matters 155

  4. Old Testament Hebrew 159

  5. Prophecy 161

  6. Divorce and Remarriage 163

  7. The Spanish Bible 165

  8. The Dean Burgon Society 167

Index of Words and Phrases 169

About the Author 185

Order Blank Pages 187

Defined King James Bible Order Form 195

The Third 200 Questions Answered By Dr. D. A. Waite

?

Introductory Considerations

Have you received your copy of *THE FIRST 200 QUESTIONS ANSWERED* (**BFT #3909 @ $12.00 + $7.00 S&H**)? Have you received your copy of *THE SECOND 200 QUESTIONS ANSWERED* (**BFT #3473 @ $12.00 + $7.00 S&H**)? If not, you might want to get a copy of each of these books and read them along with the present book of THE THIRD 200 QUESTIONS ANSWERED (**BFT #3482 @ $12.00 + $7.00 S&P**).

Though there might be questions here that were included in either the first book or the second book, they are asked by different people at different times and in different ways. My answers are also different in various ways. As in the first and second question and answer books, I have included an extensive index of both words and phrases. You might have a specific topic that you are seeking answers to. Try to find it in the index. I hope I have included it.

> # CHAPTER I
> # QUESTIONS ABOUT THE
> # NEW TESTAMENT GREEK
> # TEXTS

The Critical Text And The KJB
QUESTION #401

It is difficult to understand how godly Christian men can not understand about these textual matters, even when becoming aware of the King James only position and arguments. <u>What is it that makes them disagree? How are they looking at it from a different perspective that has them come to a different conclusion</u>?

There seems to be this area of judging and grace happening--taking the stand with the King James Bible, there does seem to be grace extended to those that are of the other perspective, because there are good works done by those people, even using the modern translations.

The Textus Receptus was used by the translators for the King James Bible. They used the Textus Receptus, which essentially represents the majority of Greek texts (the Textus Receptus would be like a heading for a file folder and then certain documents in that folder). <u>At that time, were the other texts that are used by the modern translations, available or did they surface later</u>?

Also, I need to be refreshed about Westcott and Hort. They relied on Vatican manuscript (B). Those manuscripts were found in a Catholic monastery and were used for the modern bible translations. <u>Is that correct? Did these manuscripts surface after the King James Bible translation or were those manuscripts rejected by those translators?   Also, were Vatican manuscripts used for NASB and NIV and NKJB</u>?

If I remember correctly, Erasmus put together the Greek texts that were used by the translators. Erasmus had been a Catholic and was converted and left the Catholic church, although he continued to associate with Catholics but died outside the Catholic church with people that were Protestants around his bedside (not Catholics around him). It makes it particularly interesting that Erasmus had been a Catholic and was converted and a born-again Christian and that the false texts were found in a Catholic monastery and had the name "Vatican" on them.

Also, I read the booklet about Westcott and Hort where you had printed their writings and analyzed them. I actually couldn't even understand what Westcott and Hort were saying, it seemed so convoluted.

ANSWER #401

The Greek MSS favored by the modern Critical Text followers were known by the KJB translators and were rejected by them as false and disreputable. Though the Vatican and Sinai MSS might not have been in hand, there were many "children" of these around and their readings which contradicted the vast number of other MSS that were rejected by the translators.

Part of this I answered above. "B" or Vatican was found in the Vatican library. It was Sinai (Aleph) that was found in a St. Catherine's monastery near Mt. Sinai. The Vatican and/or Sinai or both formed the basis of the ERV, NIV, NASV, ESV, RSV, NRSV, NEV, and most of the others. the NKJV was "supposedly" based on the TR, but I found at least 3 places where they used the Critical Text. Another man found over 100 places, but I have not checked this myself.

The KJB did not use Erasmus's text of 1516, but that of Beza's 5th edition, 1598, 82 years later which was similar to that of Erasmus, but had refined it and taken out any misspellings, etc. I do not believe Erasmus was born-again, but he might have been. The Pope banned his books. Erasmus did refuse a Cardinal's hat. He was buried in a Protestant cemetery. I have seen pictures of his grave in that cemetery.

I agree that the writings of Westcott and Hort were very "*convoluted.*" You are correct in this assessment.

The NA And UBS Critical Texts

QUESTION #402

1. The people make reference to the Nestle/Aland Text. Can you in any way shed some light on this? For example, I was told, "*The committee consulted the most recent edition of the United Bible Societies text.*" What is the Nestle/Aland text? How close to the originals is it? When was this text discovered and where?

2. When was this text first made up? What part of the world did these come from? Who is responsible for creating it. Why was it created?

3. Can you explain which Greek Critical Text was used in the translation of the first and subsequent NIV NT's? What was used to write this "*Critical Text*"? Where did this come from?

ANSWER #402

1. The committee for the NIV used a Critical Text, which follows either the United Bible Societies (UBS) Text or the Nestle/Aland (NA) Text. The NA Text is a combined name of a German named Nestle, the grandfather, and Aland his grandson. It is therefore called the Nestle/Aland Text.

The UBS and NA Critical Greek Texts are printed texts that you can buy and use or disuse as you please. Both Texts are based largely on the same Text as that used by Westcott and Hort in 1881. These Gnostic Critical Greek Texts vary from the Traditional Greek Words underlying the King James Bible in over 8,000 places. Each of these places can be found in Dr. Jack Moorman's book, *8,000 Differences Between The Critical Greek Text and the Traditional Greek Text* (**BFT #3084 @ $20.00 +$7.00 S&H**). The one feature that unites all three of these Gnostic Critical Greek Texts is their following (and almost worship of) the Vatican manuscript "B." That was developed in the 2nd or 3rd century from Gnostic heretics in Alexandria, Egypt. Alexandria was also the world headquarters of Gnosticism. The Gnostics, in an effort to conform the New Testament to their many heresies, changed the Traditional Greek Text which they had in their possession in many doctrinal places. I believe that most, if not all, of the 356 doctrinal passages involved were made by these Gnostic heretics. All of these 356 doctrinal passages can be found in Dr. Jack Moorman's book, *Early Manuscripts, Church Fathers, and the Authorized Version* (BFT #3230 @ $20.00 + $7.00 S&H).

2. The first basic Gnostic Critical Greek Text came from two apostate Church of England ministers, Bishop Westcott and Professor Hort (W/H). It was published in 1881. The N/A text originated in the late 1800's by two German higher critics and apostates, one of whom was named Eberhard Nestle. Kurt Aland is a grandson. Both of these texts were created by men who despised the Textus Receptus underlying the KJB.

3. The same Critical Texts (W/H, N/A, and UBS) were used in the first NIV and in the present ones with only minor differences in the subsequent Greek editions. All of these Gnostic Critical Texts, of whatever name, are founded upon the Gnostic heretical documents of the Vatican ("B") and Sinai (Aleph) manuscripts which originated in Alexandria, Egypt.

More Westcott & Hort Changes?
QUESTION #403

Well, I discovered that the *Doctored New Testament* (BFT #3138 @ $25.00 + $7.00 S&H) reveals only those passages that were altered in the Revised Greek NT and the English Revised Version (ERV) but not the changes made by the revisers preparing the NIV NASB, etc. Is this correct? Do the NIV and NASB contain additional changes in addition to the Greek textual changes introduced by Westcott and Hort?

ANSWER #403

That is correct. The Gnostic Critical Greek Text is not the only basis for modern versions changing their wording. There are over 2,000, 4,000, 6,653+ either additions, subtractions or other changes that I found in the NKJV, NASV, and NIV respectively. These detailed changes are available in print if anyone would like to see them documented. Though I have not cataloged versions such as the RSV, NRSV, ERV, NEB, LB, ESV, and other modern versions based on the Gnostic Critical Greek Text, their changes due to their false Greek text would be there together with their flawed translation technique which could account for either 2,000, 4,000, or 6,653+ instances of dynamic equivalency. The totals in this area would have to be documented before there could be absolute certainty of the totals.

Greek Or Aramaic NT?
QUESTION #404

Do you have any teachings to defend the N.T. Greek against those who say the NT was originally in Aramaic? I have encountered a few people that insist that I am wrong. I know I am not wrong.

ANSWER #404

You are not wrong. You are correct. Perhaps the best book to get the background and proof for the Greek being the language of the original New Testament rather than Aramaic is *Forever Settled* (BFT #1428) @ $20.00 + $7.00 S&H) by Dr. Jack Moorman.

From the point of evidence, there are very few Aramaic N.T. manuscripts. Currently, there are over 5,500 Greek N.T. manuscripts. Reason alone would dictate that if Aramaic were really the original language of the New Testament rather than Greek, there would be many more copies of the Aramaic New Testament than now exist.

Erasmus 1516 Or Beza 1598?

QUESTION #405

Was the 1516 Erasmus text full of doctrinal errors? Is that why Beza's 5th edition of 1598 was made?

ANSWER #405

I don't think there were "*doctrinal errors*" in Erasmus's Greek text. That is not why Beza's 5th edition of 1598 was made. Though I have never compared the two editions, I would assume that Beza's edition merely corrected a few words and some minor spellings. Both of these texts are rightly called "*Traditional Texts.*" They agree in most places. They are sister texts, despite minor variations. This is also true of the Complutensian Polyglot text, the Stephens 1550 text, and the Elzevir text. All these Greek "*Traditional Texts*" are very similar. One source, for example, estimates the differences in words between the Stephens 1550 edition and the Beza 5th edition in 1598 numbered only between 125 to 150 words out of a total of 140,521 Greek New Testament Words. This number of differences in words is far less than those found between the Gnostic Critical Text manuscripts like Vatican and Sinai and their few manuscript followers. Herman Hoskier, in his massive 924-page book, *Codex B and Its Allies* (**BFT #1643** @ $46.00 + $12.00 S&H) has shown <u>over 3,000 differences</u> between the Vatican and the Sinai manuscripts in the Gospels of Matthew, Mark, Luke, and John.

The Erasmus Contribution to TR

QUESTION #406

I'm a little confused as to the contribution of Erasmus to the Bible text issue. Was it his work, or was he only the publisher of this edition?

ANSWER #406

My understanding of the Erasmus edition is that his Greek and Latin parallel New Testament was his own work. His 1516 edition was the first to be printed, though the Complutensian Polyglot of Cardinal Ximenes was completed first. The KJB Greek text was not that of Erasmus, 1516, but the improved and updated text of Beza's 5th edition, 1598, 82 years later. Our Fundamentalist Gnostic Critical Text friends continuously lie about Erasmus's Greek edition as being the foundation of the King James Bible rather than that of Beza. I have tried to straighten out the **NT GREEK** men in the various books I have written on the subject, but to no avail. Our efforts to correct these brethren have all fallen on deaf ears. They continue to lie about the basis of our King James Bible's New Testament Words.

Gnostic Critical Text Vs. The TR
QUESTION #407

In looking at an article about the Critical Texts, there seems to be a whole lot of manuscripts (and pieces of manuscripts) with variations in them, where scribes changed the wording, added to it, and then scholars go through all those scripts and try to figure out what is actually God's Words, since there are variations from one manuscript to another.

With the Received Texts, were there a lot of variations of wording in various manuscripts where scholars had to figure out which manuscripts were closer to the original and then gathered those together to call them the Received Texts? In other words, did the King James translators gather up a lot of texts which were called the Received Texts and then have to sort through them to come up with particular manuscripts which they thought were the preserved Words of God, or were there actual manuscripts that made it unnecessary to go through that process?

ANSWER #407

A brief answer to your question is this: In 1967, Kurt Aland (a Gnostic Critical Text man) had 5,255 MSS available (there are around 300 more they have found since then). Of these 5,255, (1) there are only about 45 MSS surviving of the Gnostic Critical Text variety (less than 1% of the total); (2) there are about 5,210 MSS surviving of the Traditional Text variety (over 99% of the total).

The traditional text MSS were compiled by editors in editions such as Erasmus, Complutensian Polyglot, Stephens, Beza, Elzevir, Scrivener, etc. The KJB used 99% or more of Beza's 5th edition of 1598. This was what Dr. Frederick Scrivener put in his Greek edition. Both by faith and by fact, I have come to believe the Words that underlie the King James Bible are the Words God preserved in the N.T.

While there are minor differences in the various Traditional Greek Texts, the true readings can be readily ascertained by comparison. If 8 or 9 MSS have one reading and the other one or two have a different reading, it is easy to conclude what the true reading is. With the Gnostic Critical Greek Texts, the differences are major and overwhelming. Most of the CT men just go with Gnostic Vatican or Sinai manuscripts or both of them. When these two are in conflict, these critics usually go with Vatican ("B").

Burgon's Church Fathers' Quotes

QUESTION #408

It has come to my attention that the British Museum (allegedly) holds an unpublished work by Dean J. W. Burgon. In my thinking it warrants being retrieved for the benefit of all who hold to the principals of un-edited proof of the Greek texts in the Byzantine Common Majority Universal Antiochian tradition. I refer to an article by Ronald J. Gordon (Oct 2002) where he reports

"To Burgon's credit but locked away in the British Museum is his most ambitious and unpublished work, a detailed catalog of more than 86,000 quotations of the early Church Fathers, the only project of its kind and a companion effort to his being the only Textual Critic to personally collate the Big Five Uncials."

Are you able to advise if this document can be accessed (if not already), and what prospect maybe of being published? I feel assured that it will contain strong evidence of supporting witness to the "Byzantine" text from extant pre-4th Century MSS, thus adding substantial weight against the out-worn and eclectic claims of *"oldest and best"* Alexandrian adherents.

ANSWER #408

The 86,000 quotations of the early church fathers are still in the British Museum. They are color-coded and must be photographed in color to get the maximum benefit. According to Dr. Jack Moorman who is our MSS scholar in London, the British Museum will not let people photograph these quotations themselves. They charge quite a bit per page for their pictures. Also, we don't know the exact edition of the Church Fathers that Dean Burgon used, so the pages will not line up without having these exactly. In summary, Dr. Moorman feels we should give up on this project. I remember that Dr. David Otis Fuller had these quotations photographed in black and white film, gave them to someone, and they are now lost.

Dr. Jack Moorman has done some research on this subject. He has used the current Ante-Nicene Fathers and has re-done Burgon's analysis of the 76 church fathers who died 400 A.D. and before. From these church fathers' quotations, Dean Burgon found 60% quotes from the Traditional Text and only 40% from the Neologian (or Gnostic Critical Greek Text) quotes. In Dr. Moorman's research, he found 70% quotes from the Traditional Text and only 30% from the Gnostic Critical Text. This is available in his book, *Early MSS, Church Fathers, and the Authorized Version* (BFT #3032 @ $20.00 + $7.00 S&H.)

The "Majority Text" Refuted

QUESTION #409

Our library recently purchased Wipf & Stock's reprint of Scrivener's *Adversaria Critica Sacra*. In his introduction, Scrivener refers to his Editio Major 1887--his edition of Steven's NT of 1550.

Am I correct in assuming Editio Major 1887 is a different NT edition than Scrivener's NT in Greek (1881, 1883, 1884, 1886, 1890, 1908) which you publish as *Scrivener's Annotated Greek New Testament*?

On another note, is there any chance that Dr. Jack Moorman's book, *When the King James Bible Departs from the Majority Text* (**BFT #1617 @ $20.00 + $7.00 S&H**), could be reformatted and printed as a book? With the popularity of the NKJV it seems the need to have a hardbound edition is greater than ever.

ANSWER #409

Scrivener's edition of Steven's 1550 is different from our Scrivener's Annotated Greek New Testament which is the Greek text underlying the KJB, namely Beza's 5th edition of 1598. We do have a copy of Scrivener's Steven's 1550 in copy machine format. It is quite similar to, if not identical to, the Steven's Greek (with the footnotes and all) as found in the *Interlinear Greek N.T.* of George Ricker Berry (**BFT #186 @ $30.00 + $7.00 S&H**).

Your suggestion of putting Dr. Jack Moorman's book, *When the KJB Departs From the So-Called Majority Text* (**BFT #1617 @ $20.00 + $7.00 S&H**) into hardback or even printed in perfect binding is a good one. Dr. H. D. Williams, one of our Vice Presidents of the Dean Burgon Society has just completed the publication of this book through Print On Demand (POD).

Accurate Copies Are "Inspired Words"

QUESTION #410

When Paul told Timothy that his family had raised him on the "*holy scriptures*," and that these were "*inspired Words*," we will both surely agree that Timothy was not taught from the "*original*" OT writings, but from **copies** that were far removed from the "*originals*." And as there was no way to ascertain the accuracy of these "*copies*" to the "*originals*," yet Paul proclaims them as "*holy scripture*" that is "*inspired*" ("*God-breathed*").

How do you reconcile this fact with your statement that "*Inspired Words need not to have been given by the **process** of God's inspiration*," which, I must admit, is a definition that is new to me. 2 Timothy 3:15-16 is used as a proof-text for "*inspiration*" of the entire Bible.

ANSWER #410

I believe the Hebrew Scriptures Timothy knew were accurate copies of the original Hebrew and Aramaic originals. As such, they can be called "inspired Words" though those copies were not given by the **process** of inspiration which happened only once. The Old Testament Scriptures referred to in verse 15 were copies. The Scriptures referred to in verse 16 were the original Hebrew and Aramaic Words (and, by extension, the Greek N.T. which was being God-breathed). I see no conflict in v. 15 (which were **copies**) and v. 16 (which were **originals**).

Greek Manuscript Variances

QUESTION #411

I need information that covers the variance of the TR family (Byzantine, Stephanus, etc.), as well as will clearly express why the Westcott and Hort are not the accepted texts. If there are articles that you know of on the web, that would be great, or if you have a book and I can buy it that is fine too. I know your book on *Defending the King James Bible* goes into the textual basis some, but doesn't cover the variances of the TR, if my memory serves me correctly. Thanks.

ANSWER #411

What you **should** be interested in would be the variances between the TR and the Critical Text, rather than in the slight differences among the six or so TR's like Erasmus, the Complutensian Polyglot, Stephens, Beza, Elziver, or Scrivener. There are perhaps 125 or so small differences between some of them, but, in general, they agree. Your request sounds like the Gnostic Critical Text arguments of Bob Jones University and those of our other Fundamentalist Gnostic Critical Text friends. They say, "*well you can't trust the TR because there are 10 to 15 or more different editions of the various TR's.*"

I don't know that we have material specifically on this, but I would remind you of my own reasoning after reading and studying this theme since 1970. I don't take the Erasmus TR of 1516, but the Beza's 5th edition of 1598 (82 years later) which our KJB scholars used. They changed it slightly in 190 places, according to Dr. Frederick Scrivener as he lists them in his APPENDIX. You can get this titled *Scrivener's Annotated Greek New Testament* (**BFT #1670 @ $35.00 + $7.00 S&H**). This is the TR that I accept (by fact and by faith) as a copy of the original Greek Words. This conclusion necessitates "*an inductive leap*" as they say in the study of inductive logic. It means you accumulate as many facts as you can, fact after fact, and then you must take that "*inductive leap*" into a conclusion, even though there may be other facts you have not found.

We can't continue to doubt the source and foundation of our O.T. and N.T., but must have a solid foundation from which to translate the Words of God into all the languages of the world. As for me and my house, we take the Hebrew, Aramaic, and Greek Words underlying our King James Bible as preserved copies of the original Words. The Lord Jesus Christ promised to preserve every one of His Words (Hebrew, Aramaic, and Greek) See Psalms 12:6-7; Matthew 5:18; 24:35; Mark 13:31; and Luke 21:33. It is our task to discover those promised preserved Words that will not and have not "*passed away.*"

There comes a point at which you must agree with the saying: "*A man convinced against his will is of the same opinion still.*" Dr. Humberto Gomez based his text as clearly as he could on the Hebrew, Aramaic, and Greek Words underlying the KJB, using the Spanish 1909 wherever it was correct. The Spanish 1960 edition, on the other hand, is based on the Critical Greek text (for the most part) which varies from the TR of the KJB in over 8,000 places. This is detailed in Dr. Jack Moorman's book, *8,000 Differences Between the Critical Text And The Received Text* (*BFT #3084 @ $20.00 + $7.00 S&H*).

I haven't named a book, but I have tried to give you the thinking that should go into your mind. If you want to go "whole-hog" into the Critical Text and have been trained in this error and don't want to change for any reason, there is nothing much that can be done.

There are basically two kinds of people: (1) Those who are open to truth, seek it, and when truth is found, reject untruth, and cling to the truth. (2) Those who are not open to truth, do not seek it, and if truth is found, reject truth, and cling to the untruth. There is not much you can do with the #2 people, sad to say. I am of the #1 persuasion and changed my mind from the Critical Text to the TR after I began to research the subject. I had never been told the truth about the Greek Text controversy in Dallas Theological Seminary's Greek department. They never even mentioned the TR or Traditional Text during my five residence years from 1948 through 1953. They sold me a copy of Westcott and Hort's Greek text in their bookstore. I used it throughout my five years in that Seminary without knowing anything was wrong with it.

Westcott And Hort's O.T.

QUESTION #412

1. What did Westcott and Hort do to the (Masoretic, KJ) Old Testament in 1870-81?

2. Specifically, did they swap it for the Septuagint?

3. Could you recommend a sold reference work which would reveal their final 1881 (Greek and Hebrew) text?

ANSWER #412

1. Westcott and Hort did not "*tinker*" with the O.T. so far as I know. Dean Burgon warned that "we should not '*tinker*' the Hebrew text." They aimed their artillery on the N.T. principally. The modern versions do use the LXX in many places in the O.T.

2. Not to my knowledge. I believe they just altered the English to bring it up to what they considered to be more correct than the KJB.

3. In my book, *Defending the King James Bible* (p. xii, and in other places), here is my analysis of the W/H changes in the Greek text as to total. To get the exact places where they have changed in these 5,604 places, I would recommend our son, D. A. Waite, Jr.'s book *The Doctored New Testament* (BFT #3138 @ $25.00 + $7.00 S&H) where you can see every one of these places in **bold** type with the changes made in the footnotes.

For an even more detailed reference source where over 8,000 changes were made between the Westcott and Hort kind of Gnostic Critical Text,

THE N.T. GREEK TEXTUAL BATTLEGROUND

TEXTUS RECEPTUS	W/H CHANGES IN T.R.
Has 140,521 Greek wds.	Changes 5,604 places in the N.T.
Has 647 pp. in Greek Text	Changes include 9,970 Greek wds.
Has 217 Greek wds. per page	Changes 15.4 Greek wds. per page
Has 100% of the Greek wds.	Changes 7% of the Greek wds.
Has all 647 pp. unchanged	Changes total 45.9 pp. in Greek text

What About Bible Colophons?

QUESTION #413

My question is regarding the little notes some versions omit, and even certain publishers of KJV's omit (and I think wrongfully) at the end of all of Paul's epistles, which would include Hebrews, in my opinion. (All Cambridge Bibles I have seen have them included, for one example.) I don't know what they are called, and I know they are not Scripture, but they are valuable, historically, right? If they were included by the ancient copyists, who are we to omit them? Also, will the new Spanish version, the Reina Valera Gomez Bible, have these notes included in their text? Do you have any writings about this particular subject of the endnotes to the NT Pauline epistles?

ANSWER #413

You are correct that the Cambridge KJB's contain the colophons (as they are called). Our *Defined King James Bible* is a Cambridge text and contains these colophons. As I understand it, they were a part of the Textus Receptus manuscripts. Dr. Gomez's Spanish Bible does have these colophons as well. I don't know of a book that takes these up from our viewpoint, but this URL might be some help: http://www.skypoint.com/~waltzmn/Scribes.html if you wish to look at it.

What Are Alexandrian Manuscripts?

QUESTION #414

I am the Pastor of a Baptist Church in Georgia. I take a Textus Receptus & King James stand. I was asked by a member what MSS are in the Alexandrian Text. Could you tell me?

ANSWER #414

The leading MSS in the Alexandrian Text are the Vatican ("B") and the Sinai (Aleph) and about 43 others. They total only about 45 out of over 5,255 as of 1967. This is less than 1% of the evidence.

You and your people might be interested in my new booklet *The Superior Foundation of the King James Bible* (**BFT #3384 @ $10.00 + $6.00 S&H**) which takes up the Hebrew and Greek Words underlying it.

Origin Of The Traditional Text?

QUESTION #415

I am debating a young man that says the TR/RT was not composed until the early 1600's. How can I shoot down his argument?

ANSWER #415

Remember this true saying, "*A man convinced against his will is of the same opinion still.*" Don't think you're going to make a convert of an unwilling young man. Don't hold your breath!!

The truth of the matter (though this young man probably doesn't care to know it) is that, as Dean Burgon has said it, the Traditional, Received text has come down to us from the Apostolic times to the present. However, the printing of that text began with Erasmus in 1516. Others in the Traditional

Text tradition came along with Steven's edition 1550, Beza's 5th edition, 1598, and with others. But the manuscripts which form the basis of the various editions of the Traditional or Received text go all the way back to the originals of the N.T. which closed from 90 to 100 A.D. rather than in the *"early 1600's."*

Again, don't hold your breath that this young man will jettison the theories taught to him by his Gnostic Critical Text teachers and accept the truth of the matter, unless he is seeking truth rather than mere slanted opinion.

Bart Ehrman's False Views Refuted
QUESTION #416

Has anyone from the DBS interacted with the writings of Bart Ehrman? I have seen J Patrick Holding's reviews and read Dan Wallace's review of Ehrman on his web site but have not seen anything from the DBS. This man (Ehrman) is on a mission to evangelize for agnosticism and must not be ignored.

ANSWER #416

None of our DBS men, to my knowledge, have sought to answer Ehrman in detail, but have continuously refuted his heresies and those of his mentor, Bruce Metzger. Remember this true saying: *"A man convinced against his will is of the same opinion still."* I do not believe that anything our DBS men could say to Ehrman would change his mind on things. Do you think that he would?

Though I don't know that the Dean Burgon Society men have written on him, the following article would be a good one to look at: *From Faith To Apostasy: The Spiritual Journey of a Modern Textual Scholar* By Pastor Bradley Robert Berglund through David W. Cloud October 26, 2006.

I think you would agree that Ehrman (who was converted from Moody Bible Institute salvation to agnosticism) would not likely be converted from Bruce Metzger's textual position to that of Dean John William Burgon.

The 1 John 5:7-8 Problems Explained
QUESTION #417

I have another question on 1 John 5:7-8. The Godhead's witness of the outpouring of blood and water seems to be so strong and pointed here. However, it seems that verses 7 and 8 are clearly definable as Father, Son, and Holy Spirit. The witnesses on earth (the spirit, the water, and the blood) seem to include all Three. Would not the blood be Jesus, and the water the spirit? But then there is the Spirit. He would be witnessing twice. Which of these three would represent God the Father so that each Person of the Godhead would be represented? Or what am I missing?

ANSWER #417

I think, though it might be nice to have v. 8 be a reflection of the Trinity, I don't think this is absolutely necessary.

I think that the things on earth that bear witness to God's work on earth are God the Holy Spirit ("*Spirit*"), the Words of God ("*water*" Ephesians 5:26), and the cleansing Blood of the Lord Jesus Christ ("*blood.*")

The first three are in Heaven, the last three on earth. At least that's how I see it.

99% TR Versus 1% CT Greek MSS

QUESTION #418

Thanks for the note about the percentages of T.R. to the Critical Text. Do we have your permission to report that: "*According to the Dean Burgon Society, 99% of the manuscript evidence supports Textus Receptus, while only 1% stands in favor of the Critical Text.*" Let me know if this is acceptable.

From what I gathered of the discussion, it sounded as if Dr. Moorman had not actually reported a percentage in his book, but was only estimating when he mentioned the 93 to 7 percent in the interview -- based upon what he remembered of all the various manuscripts. It seems that you, Dr. Waite, had actually done the analysis of his data and came up with the 99 to 1 percent ratio. Have I understood this correctly?

ANSWER #418

Your statement is good, but instead of saying the "Dean Burgon Society" it would be better to say "Dr. D. A. Waite, President of the Dean Burgon Society and Director of the Bible For Today said" or something like that. These statistics are mine based on Dr. Moorman's figures in his book, *Forever Settled* (BFT #1428 @ $20.00 + $7.00 S&H).

As for the papyri which are Gnostic Critical Text (CT) versus the Textus Receptus (TR), on p. 107 of his book, Dr. Moorman says only 13 out of 88 are CT.

As for the uncials which are CT versus TR, on p. 120, Dr. Moorman says only 9 out of 267 are CT.

As for the cursives which are CT versus TR, on pp. 125-126, Dr. Moorman says only 22 out of 2401 (The *Nestle/Aland* total in 1967 was 2741 but if you use 2401, this would make CT MSS even less than using the 2741) are CT (I got 23 from somewhere, but that difference of 1 would not change the percentages.

As for the lectionaries which are CT versus TR, on p 65, Dr. Moorman gives the total of 2,143 lectionaries. I cannot find at the moment the place where he says these are 100% TR, but I must have found it in his book.

Dr. Moorman never put these figures in chart form as I have done, but again, I like to quantify data to make people see the true picture of the battle that we're in for the TR MSS versus the CT MSS. These totals are as of 1967 from Kurt Aland's figures. There are about 300 more manuscripts discovered since then, but I would imagine that the percentages would not change appreciably. In fact, the TR percentage would probably go up, since there are so many more of these that were copied through the years.

Here is my chart of comparison of the Westcott and Hort (WH) manuscripts versus the Textus Receptus (TR) manuscripts. The comparison is given both in numbers and in percentages.

	TOTALS	# of MSS	% of MSS
	WH/TR	WH/TR	WH/TR
Papyrus Fragments	81(88)	13/75	15%/85%
Uncials	267	9/258	3%/97%
Cursives	2764	23/2741	1%/99%
Lectionaries	2143	0/2143	0%/100%
TOTALS: 5255		45/5210(17)1%/99%	

Studying The Greek N.T.

QUESTION #419

I am going to start studying Greek. I would like to know which Greek text is the most trustworthy. I would value your opinion on this subject.

ANSWER #419

I recommend the Textus Receptus Greek text that underlies the King James Bible. It can be bought either as BFT #471 (**at $14.00 + $7.00 S&H**) or as BFT #1670 (**at $35.00 + $7.00 S&H**). The former is smaller print and only the text. The latter is larger print and has bold letters where the Gnostic Critical Texts have changed the Traditional Greek Text underlying the King James Bible either by adding, subtracting, or changing the words in some other way.

I also have a first and a second year Greek course on audio cassettes if you are interested in them.

1. 1260/1-37 Cassettes $150.00 N.T. Greek Course-8 Sem. Hrs. (40-2hr. cassettes.; +Grammar) (B) Waite, Dr. D. A.
2. 1064/1-30 Cassettes $80.00 Second Year Greek--Translation of John & Exegesis--30 cassettes. Waite, Dr. D. A. (Dana & Mantey textbook is extra)

My first year Greek course, including the textbook can be viewed without charge at http://www.biblefortoday.org/greek.htm if you wish to do so.

The Basis Of The Textus Receptus
QUESTION #420
What is the Textus Receptus based on? Where did it come from anyway?
ANSWER #420

The Textus Receptus or Received Text is based on the original Greek manuscripts written by the writers of the New Testament. It is made up of over 99% of the 5,255 Greek N.T. manuscripts that Kurt Aland had as of 1967. This percentage is figured from Dr. Jack Moorman's research as recorded in his book, *Forever Settled* (**BFT #1428** @ **$20.00+ $7.00 S&H**).

Though there are over 300 more manuscripts that have been found since 1967, it is assumed that the percentages are comparable to those found in 1967. The Received Text that I believe is the correct one, is the text that underlies the King James Bible. It is based on Beza's 5th edition of 1598 as printed by Dr. Frederick Scrivener. Dean John William Burgon called this the Traditional Text which he proves to have continuity from the Apostolic times to the present.

The Received Greek N.T. text is to be distinguished sharply from the Gnostic Critical Text which is the text followed by most of the textual critics today and used as the basis for most of the modern versions in all languages. It is based on less than 1% of the manuscript evidence. I believe this is a false text based on the Gnostic documents of the Vatican and Sinai manuscripts from Alexandria, Egypt, which had been perverted by false Gnostic doctrines. It differs from the Traditional Greek Words underlying the King James Bible in over 8,000 places. These places are shown in Dr. Jack Moorman's book entitled *8,000 Differences Between The Critical Greek Text and the Received Greek Text* (**BFT #3084** @ **$20.00 + $7.00 S&H**).

Is There A Reliable Interlinear TR?
QUESTION #421
I've been searching high & low for a **reliable** interlinear Textus Receptus (TR) that doesn't contain any corrupt readings. Do you know of any & where I could obtain a copy?
ANSWER #421
I don't know of any interlinear of the TR at this time. There are two interlinear New Testaments, but both have certain defects. I think they both have their usefulness, but I don't know whether or not you would consider them

to be "*reliable*." If you had asked for New Testament interlinears that were close to the TR, I would have listed them for you.

"Majority" Text And TR Differences

QUESTION #422

How many differences are there between the "*Majority Text*" and the "*Textus Receptus*"?

ANSWER #422

The so-called "*Majority Text*" differs from the "*Textus Receptus*" in 1500 to 1800 places. There are at least two different "*Majority Texts*": (1) one by Zane Hodges and Arthur Farstad, and (2) one by Robinson and Pierpont. I understand that Wilbur Pickering might have even a third one, but I do not have a copy of that one.

The Greek Text Of F. H. A. Scrivener

QUESTION #423

Would you tell me if Scrivener's Greek is in a book that follows the same format as that of *The Englishman's Greek New Testament*.

ANSWER #423

Scrivener's Annotated Greek New Testament (all in Greek) is not exactly the same format as Englishman's Greek NT, but it is close.

In *Scrivener's Annotated*, the places where the Gnostic Critical Greek Text words are used rather than the Textus Receptus are in bold. Then, at the bottom of the page (like Englishman's) there is the way that the Gnostic words have either added, subtracted, or changed the TR words.

Our son, D. A. Waite, Jr., has done a similar thing in English using the King James Bible rather than the Greek New Testament. It is called *The Doctored New Testament*. The Greek words in the footnotes are transliterated so English readers can read them.

37 Historical Links For The TR

QUESTION #424

I have recently discovered your website and have really enjoyed watching both your church services and many of the DBS video's. I must admit that others in the KJV camp have been detrimental to the cause due to their over-the-top rhetoric and accusations, and lack of scholarly work on the subject. I'm not saying that there are not those who have put scholarly work into the subject. I have been very impressed by the work of Dr. Branine, Dr.

Hollowood, and the black pastor, Mr. Sutton, as well as your own.

I recently purchased your book, *Defending the King James Bible*, in the hopes of examining the subject more closely for myself. That is the first book I've purchased from the KJV viewpoint. My main question is as follows: In your book there is the section entitled *Thirty-Seven Historical Evidences Supporting the Textus Receptus*. However, much of what follows are simply assertions on your part with no corroborating documentation, footnotes, or other ways to examine your claims. Can you give me references that I may examine the claims that you make? I have recently begun to use the TR in my own translating as I prepare for my messages, and I've done so because of you and your fellow speakers. Thank you for your ministry. I will continue to receive your sound instruction on your website, and I look forward to any help you can offer on this subject.

ANSWER #424

I am glad you were able to view our website and view our services and DBS videos. The reason I included the 37 historical evidences for the TR is that when speaking at a Baptist church to their deacons, one asked me if I had any evidence that the TR was used in an unbroken succession from apostolic times to the present. I found these 37 links somewhere, but do not remember where. I took for granted that this lineage was correct.

##15-37 can be easily ascertained as being true. ##1-14 I believe will be shown to be true as well upon examination. This argument does not impress the CT people even if all 37 historical TR links are proven to be true. They simply say that all of the historic churches were wrong and they should have followed the Vatican and Sinai manuscripts (which number about 45 out of 5,255 as of 1967, while the TR MSS number about 5,210.) This less than 1% vs. more than 99% still doesn't impress the CT believers. They simply say that the Vatican and Sinai are older hence closer to the original dates, therefore perfect. They do not believe that the Gnostics of Alexandria, Egypt, corrupted these two Alexandrian MSS in at least 8,000 places with at least 356 doctrinal passages which are unorthodox.

Here are thirty-seven historical evidences supporting the continuity of the Traditional Received Text of the New Testament referred to above:

13.   The Thirty-Seven Historical Evidences Supporting the Textus Receptus. Here are the thirty-seven links in the chain of historical evidence to support the Received Text.

a.   Historical Evidences for the Received Text During the Apostolic Age (33--100 A.D.)

(1)All of the Apostolic Churches used the Received Text.

(2)   The churches in Palestine used the Received Text.

(3)   The Syrian Church at Antioch used the Received Text.

b.   **Historical Evidences for the Received Text During the Early Church Period (100--312 A.D.)**

Dr. Scrivener and Dean Burgon both agree that, during the first 100 years after the New Testament was written, the greatest corruptions took place to the Received Text used by the early church. The B (Vatican) and Aleph (Sinai) manuscripts and the approximately forty-three allies which underlie the Westcott-and-Hort-type text were, I believe, the result of such corruptions.

Some of the heretics which operated in this period were Marcion, (160 A. D.); Valentinus, (about 160 A. D.); Cyrinthus, (50-100 A. D.); Sabellius, (about 260 A. D.); and others.

(4)   The Peshitta Syriac Version, (150 A. D., the second century.)   This was based on the Received Text.

(5)   Papyrus #66 used the Received Text.

(6)   The Italic Church in Northern Italy (157A. D.) used the Received Text.

(7)   The Gallic Church of Southern France (177 A.D.) used the Received Text.

(8)   The Celtic Church in Great Britain used the Received Text.

Why did all these have their Bibles based on the Received Text?--the churches in Italy, France, and Great Britain--WHY? Because those were the true Words of God, and they knew it. That was the Received Text. They lived in 150 A. D. The Bible was completed in 90-100 A. D. They had the originals right there in their hands and they based it on that which was pure, accurate, and preserved by God and by the Lord Jesus Christ Who preserves everything. These churches used this text and not any other.

The heretics made most of the changes in the Received Text during this time; the greatest proportion of which, according to both Dr. Scrivener and Dean Burgon, were made during the first 100 years after they were originally written.

(9)   Church of Scotland and Ireland used the Received Text.

(10) The Pre-Waldensian churches used the Received Text.

(11) The Waldensians (120 A. D. and onward) used the Received Text.

c.   Historical Evidences for the Received Text During the Byzantine Period (312--1453 A.D.)

(12) The Gothic Version of the 4th century used the Received Text.

(13) Codex W of Matthew in the 4th or 5th century used the Received Text.

(14) Codex A in the Gospels (in the 5th century) used the Received Text.

(15) The vast majority of extant New Testament manuscripts all used the Received Text. This includes about 99% of them, or about 5,210 of the 5,255 MSS.

(16) The Greek Orthodox Church used the Received Text.

We don't agree with many of their doctrines or practices, but that entire church for over 1,000 years has used the Received Text. Why? They know the Greek language. They're Greeks. Even though they are modern Greeks, they use the New Testament that is based upon the Received Text because it is the Words of God, and they know it.

(17) The present Greek Church still uses the Received Text.

When Mrs. Waite and I were in Israel, we visited the church which is supposed to be on the place where Jesus was born, the Church of the Nativity. They have a big Church built on the site. It doesn't look anything like the original place, I am certain. I don't even think it is on the proper place. They have commercialized it. In Jerusalem, they have Christ born in various places, crucified in various places, and buried in several places. In the Church of the Nativity, Christ's supposed birth place, we met a Greek Orthodox priest. I said to him, "You're a member of the Greek Orthodox clergy, is that right?" He said, "Yes," and then told us his name. I said, "You have a New Testament you use, don't you?" "Oh, yes," he said. I asked, "Which text do you use? Are you familiar with the so-called Westcott-and-Hort-type-text?" "*Oh, yes,*" he said,

> "*We use the Received Text; we have no confidence at all in the Westcott and Hort text.*"

That was interesting. The Greek Orthodox Church still goes back to this text that underlies the KING JAMES BIBLE.

d.   Historical Evidences for the Received Text During the Early Modern Period (1453--1831 A.D.)

(18) The churches of the Reformation all used the

Received Text.

(19) The Erasmus Greek New Testament (1516) used the Received Text.

(20) The Complutensian Polyglot (1522) used the Received Text.

A Roman Catholic Cardinal named Ximenes, edited it, yet it was based, not on the texts which most Roman Catholic Bibles used, the Westcott and Hort text, but on the Received Text.

(21) Martin Luther's German Bible (1522) used the Received Text.

(22) William Tyndale's Bible, (1525), used the Received Text.

Tyndale was a great Bible translator who was martyred because of his Bible translation.

(23) The French Version of Oliveton (1535) used the Received Text.

(24) The Coverdale Bible (1535) used the Received Text.

(25) The Matthews Bible (1537) used the Received Text.

(26) The Taverners Bible (1539) used the Received Text.

(27) The Great Bible (1539-41) used the Received Text.

(28) The Stephanus Greek New Testament (1546-51) used the Received Text.

(29) The Geneva Bible (1557-60) used the Received Text.

(30) The Bishops' Bible (1568) used the Received Text.

(31) The Spanish Version (1569) used the Received Text.

(32) The Beza Greek New Testament (1598) used the Received Text.

That is the Greek text that the KING JAMES BIBLE was based on, using the 1598, 5th edition of Beza.

(33) The Czech Version (1602) used the Received Text.

(34) The Italian Version of Diodati (1607) used the Received Text.

(35) The KING JAMES BIBLE (1611) used the Received Text.

(36) The Elzevir Brothers' Greek New Testament

(1624) used the Received Text.
(37) The Received Text in the New Testament is
the Received Text--the text that has survived
in continuity from the beginning of the New
Testament itself. It is the only accurate
representation of the originals we have today!

In fact, it is my own personal conviction and belief, after studying this subject since 1971, that the WORDS of the Received Greek and Masoretic Hebrew texts that underlie the KING JAMES BIBLE are the very WORDS which God has PRESERVED down through the centuries, being the exact WORDS of the ORIGINALS themselves. As such, I believe they are INSPIRED WORDS. I believe they are PRESERVED WORDS. I believe they are INERRANT WORDS. I believe they are INFALLIBLE WORDS. This is why I believe so strongly that any valid translation MUST be based upon these original language texts, and these alone!

Which Is Older--The TR Or The CT?

QUESTION #425

Do you have any evidence for the Textus Receptus being dated older than the Alexandrian Text? Because, to me, the whole argument is based on this issue of which manuscript is older. James White says the Alexandrian Texts are older. Pastor Waite says Textus Receptus is older.

ANSWER #425

The early Christians had and used the Traditional Greek New Testament manuscripts. When the Christians were burned, their Bibles were burned also. Also, since the Christians used their Bibles very much, they were torn and had to be re-copied carefully.

The date of the material on which a document is written is not the important point, it is rather the date of the Words that document contains. The Textus Receptus' Words were from the Apostolic times themselves, though the material on which they are written is younger. The Gnostic Vatican and Sinai manuscripts, though older, are filled with 8,000 differences and 356 doctrinal perversions.

This is the same argument that the non-KJV camp always uses. The Sinaiticus and Vaticanus manuscripts that the occultists Westcott and Hort used to translate into the Revised Version of 1881 are most likely older than the Textus Receptus. The reason for this is twofold (1) their disuse enabled them to be preserved; (2) the climate of Alexandria, Egypt was also conducive for their preservation. Copying of these Gnostic Alexandrian Vatican and Sinai manuscripts ceased in about 500 or 600 A.D. because the Christians knew them to contain many false words and to eliminate many true Words. Because of these Gnostic heresies the early Christians rejected these false manuscripts. This accounts for there being only about 45 manuscripts out of 5,255 (less than 1%) which have been preserved from these Gnostic sources. Over 99% of the preserved manuscripts go along with the Traditional Text Words underlying the King James Bible.

Dean Burgon's Church Fathers' Work

QUESTION #426

Can Dean Burgon's work on the church fathers be published and used today for all to see?

ANSWER #426 (By Dr. Jack Moorman)

From time to time I receive letters regarding Dean Burgon's work concerning the church fathers. The following is a recent reply to an inquiry and I think explains why I have not personally undertaken this project.

Just to put it in a little perspective, I have quoted here what Brother Dunn would like to do, and then the account I had given of my trip in 1992 to see Burgon's index, and of the main source he used - J. P. Migne's collection of quotations.

1. I share your desire to see the publishing an exhaustive list of the name of the church father and what book, chapter and verse that he quoted, as well as the quote itself.

2. I would prefer that the pages be purchased electronically. That is, a high resolution, color scanned image of each page would be extremely useful to both of us. To you, because you could quickly publish the work and to me, because I could use Optical Character Recognition and turn it into a very large text document, usable by a computer program.

DEAN BURGON'S INDEX

In 1992, I [Dr. Moorman] went to the then British Museum Library to see the Index. It is contained in sixteen massive volumes, which Burgon worked on between the years 1872-88 (the year of his death). The work is not a collection of patristic quotations, but rather an index giving the source of 86,489 quotations in other editions (mainly Migne). Each set of references, containing the chapter and verse of Scripture, followed by the volume and page where it is found in an edition, are pasted on the page in Biblical order under each Father. Burgon used color coding on the slips to indicate information about each quotation. Many colors were used, and thus any reproduction of the work would have to be in color. Quotations from 76 Fathers, covering the entire New Testament are referenced.

At the beginning of each Father there is a book-by-book tabulation giving the total number of quotations. I did not, however, see summaries of the times a Father quoted for or against the TR. Miller, no doubt, by interpreting and counting the colored slips, gives such a summary for the Gospels in his *Traditional Text* (pp. 99-121) (**BFT #1159 @ $15.00 + $7.00 S&H**). These show a 3/2 margin to the TR.

J. P. MIGNE'S COLLECTION OF QUOTATIONS

Migne, a French Catholic, scholar, and professor, was also something of a maverick. After getting into trouble with his bishop over a book he wrote on "priestly liberty," he moved to Paris in 1833. There he established a publishing company, which, with a large staff of editors and printers, churned out enormous amounts of ecclesiastical literature. It is his *Patrologiae Cursus Completus* which to this day remains the most extensive collection of patristic material in print. It includes works from the early Fathers to writers of the Middle Ages. The Latin Series contains 221 volumes, and the Greek 167 volumes. Scripture quotations from the Latin Series as well as the Greek move strongly toward the Received Text. Therefore, with respect to the text of Scripture, if Catholicism is to defeat "*the paper pope*" of the Protestants, it will have to look to some other means than this!

Migne came into disfavor with the archbishop of Paris: the official reason was that "*he was making too much money.*" In 1868 his establishment burned to the ground, and in 1874 a Vatican decree forbade any continuation of the work.

Despite many later disclaimers about not being a "*critical edition,*" Migne's work gives a powerful demonstration that the text of the Latin West is not that much different from the hated Received Text. For centuries, this fact made no difference as Rome kept the Bible from her people. If she is to undermine Europe's faith in the Reformation Bible, she must look for a different engine of war. Rome was prepared to look for such a weapon in the radical Aleph-B text, even though it meant declaring works like those massive patristic collections to be obsolete. In fact she has distanced herself so completely from Migne's Series that many do not realize it is a Catholic production.

If the British Library is able to produce a color scan, a digital copy of Burgon's Index would certainly be valuable for historical purposes. But it is only an index, and unfortunately does not contain the quotations themselves. To insert these, would probably mean that much of Migne's enormous work itself would have to be scanned. That definitely would take a few weeks.

With his computer expertise, Brother Dunn should probably deal directly with the British Library and see what they are prepared to do. The cost for a microfilm copy (apparently no color) back in 1992 was, with a stronger dollar, about $ 1700.00.

The *"Index of texts of the New Testament quoted by the Fathers 1872-1888"* is listed under the Manuscript Catalogue of the British Library. The Shelf Number is Add. 33421 - 33436
                   From Dr. Jack Moorman
            Dean Burgon Society Advisory Council Member
            Author and Baptist Pastor in the United Kingdom

Greek Helps In MP-3 Format?
QUESTION #427

I think you mentioned in KJB Seminar #10 that a course was available in MP-3 format on Hebrew and another in Greek. I don't see those on your website. Please tell me where to look.

ANSWER #427

These MP-3 courses are available for $25 each for Greek 1st year and Greek 2nd year and Hebrew 1st year plus the textbook costs. They are not on the Website at this time. These are the descriptions of the three courses that we have available for first and second year Greek and first year Hebrew:

BFT #1260/1-37, Cassettes, $150.00, First Year Greek Course 8 Semester Hours, 37-2-hour Cassettes; 74 hours (Textbook included), by Dr. D. A. Waite

BFT #1064/1-30, Cassettes, $80.00, Second Year Greek--Translating John & Exegesis, 30-2-hour Cassettes; 60 hours, by Dr. D. A. Waite

BFT #1162/1-40, Cassettes, $175.00, First Year Biblical Hebrew Course, 40-2-hour Cassettes; 80 hours, by Dr. D. A. Waite

W&H & Nestle/Aland Greek Texts
QUESTION #428

Thank you again for your solid ministry and for defending the KJB. I'm writing to ask if the W & H Greek New Testament is the same as the various editions of the Nestle/Aland's text. Also, what are the best representative Greek texts that a layman like myself can obtain that are the closest to the KJB Greek text & the Westcott & Hort (W/H) Greek text for comparison? I have heard that F. H. A. Scrivener's TR is the closest and an edition of Nestle's is the closest to Westcott and Hort. I do own the J. P. Green's Interlinear Hebrew, Greek, and English (which is Scrivener's TR). I have the George Ricker Berry interlinear. I also have a KJV & NIV interlinear that follows the 21st edition of Nestle's. Are these sufficient, representative sources of the original language texts?

ANSWER #428

For the TR, Scrivener's text is the best, and closest to the Words underlying the KJB and to the original Words themselves.

The W/H words are very similar to either the Nestle/Aland or the United Bible Societies Texts since all three of them are based on manuscripts Vatican ("B") and Sinai (Aleph). There is a mathematical maxim that applies here as well: "*Things equal to the same thing are equal to each other.*" They are very similar, though there are some minor changes. You can buy NA 27 or UBS 4th from their publishers if you want to spend your money that way.

You can see over 5,600 places of differences between the TR and the Gnostic Critical Greek Text with *Scrivener's Annotated Greek Text* (**BFT #1670 for $35.00 + $7.00 S&H**). This shows the places of difference in **bold** letters and puts the changes in the footnotes. If you want to have such differences in English and using the King James Bible, you can get D. A. Waite, Jr.'s *Doctored New Testament* (**BFT #3138 @ $25.00+ $7.00 S&H**).

You can also get Dr. Jack Moorman's *8,000 Differences Between the Critical Greek Text and the Textus Receptus* (**BFT #3084 @ $20.00 + $7.00 S&H**). This book shows these differences in English and in Greek. Though some of these differences are minor, there are at least 356 that are doctrinal passages which are very important differences.

Why The Critical Greek Text?
QUESTION #429
My pastor is being trained and schooled in the Critical Greek Text underlying NIV. Why is he being trained with this Greek Text?
ANSWER #429
Most Christian colleges and seminaries (like Dallas Theological Seminary where I went) believe and teach their students that the Westcott and Hort Gnostic Critical Greek text (or the Nestle/Aland or the United Bible Societies Texts) that underlie the NIV, NASV, RSV, etc. are superior and the Textus Receptus (Received Text) that underlies the KJB is defective. This training has colored probably 95% or more of the pastors and teachers in the world today.

A Free Course In 1st Year Greek
QUESTION #430
1. Do you know where I could take a correspondence course on Greek?
2. Brother Tom Gaudet in Thailand is in desperate need of a printer in Korea, can you help with any information on one?

ANSWER #430

1. My own course in 1st year Greek is available on MP-3 disks (one each). Our son, Dan, has put up this course on our Bible For Today Website (BibleForToday.org). Both the course and the textbook are found on the following LINK: http://www.biblefortoday.org/greek.htm if you want to view it. I taught very sharp students who were all college graduates. I recorded the classes on audio tape. We used Hershey Davis's text, *Beginning Greek Grammar* for the 1st year. We used Dana and Mantey's *Manual Grammar of the Greek N.T.* for the 2nd year. We also translated the entire Gospel of John. This 2nd year Greek course is available as follows:

BFT #1064/1-30 Cassettes $80.00   Second Year Greek--Translation of John & Exegesis; 30 cassettes, Waite, Dr. D. A. The text book is extra.

I'm sure there are other courses, but I'm not aware of which ones would be sound and which unsound. In my course, I stood repeatedly for the TR and KJB, though some parts of the text were on the critical text side of things.

2. Tom Gaudet might use our printer in South Korea who prints our *Defined King James Bibles*. It is called SPT. Their E-mail address is: kimyg3406@hotmail.com if you want to write them. The SPT owner is Mr. H. S. Cho. They have done a good and honest job for us in the printing of over 56,000 Bibles. If they make an error, they correct it. by giving us replacement Bibles at their next printing.

Pastors Are Trained In Critical Text
QUESTION #431

Are pastors being trained and schooled in the Critical Text underlying the NIV?

ANSWER #431

Most Christian colleges and seminaries (like Dallas Theological Seminary where I went) believe and teach their students that the Gnostic Westcott and Hort Critical Greek Text (or the Nestle/Aland or the United Bible Societies Texts) that underlie the NIV, NASV, RSV, ESV, etc. are superior and the Textus Receptus (Received Text) that underlies the KJB is defective. This training has colored probably 95% or more of the pastors and teachers in the world today.

"Majority" Versus Received Texts

QUESTION #432

1. Does that mean you no longer support the Majority Text; just the TR, or when the MT agrees with the TR?

2. How many pages are in the TR work you recommended?

3. I notice that Burgon's masterpiece, *Revision Revised*, is offered as BFT # 0470 & BFT # 0611. What's the difference between them?

4. The work recommended against the MT is against the Hodges/Farstad edition, but the only thing I've found against the Robinson/Pierpont edition is a cassette (BFT # 2490-1). The latter agrees on most departures from the KJV/TR & employs the detestable square brackets (which the former doesn't); This is the fence-sitting so favored by the pro-Egyptian texts. Doesn't this warrant a similar treatment?

5. Finally, BFT # 2483 is described as Jerome's Latin Vulgate NT. However, except for the papal Nova Vulgata (Latin translation of Egyptian Greek text), they all claim to be Jerome's. Which edition is this following? (I don't suppose it's the Rome edition of 1989 is it?)

ANSWER #432

1. I support only the Hebrew, Aramaic, and Greek Words underlying the KJB which are TR.

2. There are 656 pages in *Scrivener's Annotated New Testament*.

3. BFT #0611 is the full *Revision Revised* book. BFT #0470 is a different title.

4. Probably it does, but who has the time and interest to write it? I would be glad to publish such a detailed critique of the Robinson/Pierpont so-called "Majority Text" if someone analyzed it carefully.

5. I don't know which edition this Latin Vulgate is, but it is not the 1989. It is an older edition of the Latin Vulgate.

Greek Original N.T.--Not Aramaic

QUESTION #433

http://www.aramaicpeshitta.com has a free PDF book that has changed my view of the NT forever. The core thesis is, the New Testament was originally written in Aramaic (the native language of every last author of the NT) and then immediately translated into Greek. This translation was imperfect. Comparison with the Peshitta (the Aramaic New Testament) clears up many, many, many ambiguities, contradictions, bad idiom transfers, and anti-Jewish sentiments that exist in the Greek. Do you agree with this?

ANSWER #433

If indeed the N.T. was originally written in Aramaic, where are the thousands and thousands of copies of this original as compared with over 5,255 to 5,500 copies of the Greek in which it was originally written? That's a hard sell. The Peshitta was written in about 150 A.D. I do not believe the New Testament was written in Aramaic, but in Greek.

The NKJV's Greek Text

QUESTION #434

What text was the Greek foundation for the King James Bible's New Testament? Where did that foundation originate?

ANSWER #434

William Combs and other Fundamentalists who despise the Textus Receptus (T.R.) in favor of the Gnostic Critical Text, teach that the T.R. **originated** in 1633 because that Latin comment was found in the 1633 Elzevir's Greek New Testament. This is totally false. That Traditional Received Text **originated**, not in 1633, but in the Apostolic times when the New Testament was written. Elzevir's comment merely stated that this Apostolic Text is the Text that had been received by all.

Facts About The Textus Receptus

QUESTION #435

I was looking at a website that picked apart the Textus Receptus. Where can I find resources on the facts of the Textus Receptus, which I can print out and keep.

ANSWER #435

You can go to our BibleForToday.org site and find many of our materials in defense of the Textus Receptus. You can also go to DeanBurgonSociety.org for many more materials defending the King James Bible and its underlying Hebrew, Aramaic, and Greek Words. I would suggest you order my *Defending the King James Bible* (BFT #1594 @ $12.00 + $700). In the back of that book are listed over 1,000 other titles in defense of the KJB and its underlying Words. Some of these titles are on our Brochure #1 which we can send you without charge if you write us for it.

Analysis Of The 8,000 Differences
QUESTION #436

I recently received the *8000 Differences* book. I went through it and found 1012 words added, 3654 words deleted, giving a net loss of 2642 words. On the Dean Burgon website, I found that there were 140,521 Greek words in Scriveners Textus Receptus. 2642 divided by 140,521 equals a loss of 1.88%. It may not sound significant, but if Sydney International Airport had a 98.12% successful landing rate, 4 planes a day would crash into Botany Bay. Extrapolate that if you will to any US International Airport. Is this a good analogy?

ANSWER #436

The analogy is good, but it seems like you are misunderstanding the significance of what some of these additions and/or changes really mean. The heretics of Alexandria, Egypt, represented by manuscripts Vatican and Sinai (on which the new versions are based) have at least 356 doctrinal passages which change true doctrines into false doctrines. It is not only the quantity of the changes that are involved. It is quite often the quality of the changes which outweighs the quantity in importance. We must realize the difference between quantity and quality. Another thing this 8,000 Book proves is this. The Fundamentalists who hold to the Gnostic Critical Greek Text are writing and speaking a lie concerning changes between the Greek texts. They say the following two things: (1) They say that there are little or no differences in their Gnostic Critical Greek Text compared to the TR. They are calling over 8,000 differences either "*little*" or "*none at all*." (2) They also say that there are few or no doctrinal changes in their Gnostic Critical Greek Text vs. the TR. They are calling 356 doctrinal differences either "*few*" or "*none at all*." Both of these assertions are totally false and are proved to be wrong by the evidence contained in the *8,000 Differences* book (**BFT #3084 @ $20.00 + $7.00 S&H**).

Date Of MSS Words Vs. Materials
QUESTION #437

What percentage of the Greek New Testament (Textus Receptus) can be verified or constructed by all of the evidences we have which are dated earlier than the Alexandrian, codex vaticanus and codex sinaiticus manuscripts which are unreliable?

Also is the *Greek New Testament According to the Majority Text* used for NKJV reliable? When was it published?

ANSWER #437

Though the dates of the material on which the Words were written might not be "*dated earlier than the Alexandrian*" manuscripts, the Words themselves are earlier. They go back to the Apostolic period of the originals.

As far as manuscript evidence is concerned, over 99% of the evidence from the 5,255 manuscripts Kurt Aland had in 1967 dispute the Alexandrian manuscripts. There have been about 300 more MSS found since then, but I would assume the percentage would remain the same. Dr. Moorman's *Forever Settled* (BFT #1428 @ $20.00 + $7.00 S&H) is the source on this percentage.

The NKJV claims to have used the TR, though I found, by accident, at least three places for the Gnostic Critical Text. One person found more than 100 examples of using that text, but I have not checked on all of these.

The so-called "*Majority Text*" is not reliable, though better than the critical text. There are at least three of these (1) The one by Hodges and Farstad; (2) the one by Robinson and Pierpont; and (3) the one by Wilbur Pickering. For an accurate analysis of the so-called "*Majority Text*," you should get a copy of Dr. Jack Moorman's *Hodges and Farstad's Majority Text Refuted* (BFT #1617 @ $20.00 + $7.00 S&H).

The Brackets In Dr. Moorman's Book

QUESTION #438

Hello. I have recently been reading Dr. Moorman's fascinating book, *8,000 Differences Between the Critical Greek Text and the Received Greek Text* (BFT # 3084 @ $20.00 + $7.00 S&H). I have, however, been unable to figure out what the book means when, for the Nestle-Aland side, it has some Greek words and/or English words in parenthesis or brackets accordingly. Any light you could shine on this issue would be greatly appreciated! Right now I am looking at Mark 13:27, which translated for the Nestle-Aland says, "*and shall gather together [his] elect*"

ANSWER #438

That bracket (for English) and the parenthesis (for the Nestle-Aland Greek Text) means that they have omitted "*his*" from their text, whereas the Textus Receptus has included "*his*."

Papyrus MSS--Are They TR Or CT?

QUESTION #439

You and Pastor Moorman say many of the Papyrus MSS are Byzantine; Dr James White says none of them are Byzantine. How can a layman such as myself know who is correct.

I want to resolve this issue once and for all based solely on the facts, but how can a layman be sure of the facts/truth of the matter? I would appreciate a brief answer to this one.

ANSWER #439

On pages 106 and 107 of Dr. Jack Moorman's book, *Forever Settled* (**BFT #1428 @ $20.00 + $7.00 S&H**) lists only 13 Gnostic Critical Greek Text papyrus manuscripts. You can go to pages 103-110 for an in-depth study of these manuscripts. I would urge you not to take James White's word for anything on this subject. He despises the Textus Receptus. He follows the Gnostic Critical Greek Text line taught by his teachers at Fuller Theological Seminary and other schools where he attended. He remains dedicated to this erroneous Greek Text. He did not switch from the Westcott and Hort Greek Text that I was taught at Dallas Theological Seminary to the Traditional Greek Text that underlies the King James Bible like I did in 1970. Of course, you are free to take White's views if you wish. I prefer to side with a strong and well documented TR/KJB scholar like Dr. Jack Moorman now in England. He is one of our church's missionaries and a member of the Executive Committee of the Dean Burgon Society.

What Is Scrivener's Greek Text

QUESTION #440

Is there proof for the following statement? I have repeatedly heard this statement being made, but no proof either way to its refutation or validity. Any help you might have would be greatly appreciated. Here's the statement:

"This Greek text (Scrivener 1881) is the Greek text which corresponds best to the 1611 King James Version. The Scrivener text is a modified Beza 1598 Textus Receptus in which changes have been made to reflect the readings chosen by the KJV translators. Scrivener's intent was to artificially create a Greek text that closely matched the translator-modified Textus Receptus text and the resulting English version. This is a useful text for comparison for those with proficiency in Greek."

ANSWER #440

This is totally false. Dr. Scrivener's mission was to provide a Greek text underlying the KJB and noting with BOLD TYPE those places where the English Revised Version (ERV) of 1881 and Westcott and Hort had changed these Greek Words. Dr. Scrivener took the Greek Words of Beza's 5th edition, 1598, and printed that edition of the Greek New Testament. He found only 190 places where the KJB translators chose a different source for their words. This 190 number is a minute fraction of variation of Beza when compared to the nearly 800,000 words in the Greek N.T. Variations of this lie have been found in a number of places that I have seen. You can get the *Scrivener's Annotated Greek Text* from us as **BFT #1670 @ $35.00 + $7.00 S&H** if you wish. The 190 alleged departures from Beza's 5th edition 1598 Greek Text are in the Appendix of this volume.

CHAPTER II
QUESTIONS ABOUT
THEOLOGICAL PROBLEMS

The Ecumenical Movement
QUESTION #441

I want to ask you a question about the ecumenical movement. What are they up to now? And how can we arm ourselves against these foes or Antichrists? It seems as though no one wants to call these enemies of our Lord Jesus Christ what Christ calls them. People seem to accept anything that calls itself *"Christian"* or tags the name of Christ to it without *"trying the spirits"* to see if they are of God. I need the proof to at least show them what I am saying and hopefully the Lord will open their blind eyes.

ANSWER #441

It is difficult to convince a person against his will, even though the facts are clear. The Ecumenical movement will not stop until they have *"united"* every religion (both good, bad, and horrible) under the one Antichrist who will oppose the Bible and the Bible's Saviour. God says of these unbelievers that we are to *"Come out from among them and by ye separate."* (2 Corinthians 6:17)

Independent Baptist Churches
QUESTION #442

My first question is: Why does there seem to be two types of Christians? There are the "independent fundamental Baptist Bible believers," and then there are all the other Christians.

My second question is: Why don't all professing Christians eventually end up using and standing for the King James Version of the Bible? Then, why don't they all eventually end up at the doorstep of an independent Baptist Bible-believing church?

ANSWER #442

Question #1: I think it is individual preference. All groups think they are following the New Testament. Of course, I favor the independent fundamental Baptist church emphasis that stands for Biblical separation, the King James Bible, and the Hebrew, Aramaic, and Greek Words that underlie it.

Question #2: Many of their pastors, like I was, have been taught that the false Gnostic Critical Greek Text and the false versions are the best. They have either never been told the other side, or having been told, they prefer to hold to their false position.

The Error of "Limited Atonement"
QUESTION #443

What is your position on Christ's death? Please send me an e-mail and let me know your position regarding "*limited atonement.*" If you are an Arminian or a semi-Pelagian, I cannot support you.

ANSWER #443

I do not believe in "*limited atonement*" (that is, Christ died only for a limited group of people called the "*elect*"). I believe this is a false and an unscriptural doctrine which is leading many astray in these days. I believe, with Dr. Lewis Sperry Chafer, founder of the Dallas Theological Seminary, in "*unlimited atonement*" (that is, Christ died for the sins of the entire world, past, present, and future). I believe this, not because it was taught by Dr. Chafer, but because it is clearly taught repeatedly in the New Testament Scriptures. John the Baptist had it right when he looked at the Lord Jesus Christ and exclaimed, "*Behold the Lamb of God, which taketh away the sin of the world*" (John 1:29). John 3:16, and many other verses, makes it clear that, not just the "*elect*" can believe on the Lord Jesus Christ, but "*whosoever believeth in Him should not perish, but have everlasting life.*" From my answer, I would think you cannot "*support*" me.

Did Catholics Make The Canon?
QUESTION #444

On page 217 of your book, *Defending the King James Bible*, you state: "*In 325 A.D., the Council of Nicea determined which canonical books should be followed and which were spurious and not to be followed.*"

This, to me, would indicate that you believe that the Catholic church determined the books that should be in the NT. Is that right?

ANSWER #444

Though the Roman Catholic Church (RCC) claims to have begun during the life of Peter, it did not have its absolute way over things in 325 A.D. at Nicea. During the first 300 years, Christians were persecuted by Rome. When Constantine called this Council at Nicea in 325 A.D., the Roman Catholic system was not established.

The Apocrypha was not included in this canon of books. This is one indication, among many, that the church leaders of that day were not all Roman Catholics in sympathy. If indeed, as you imply, the Roman Catholic Church determined the books of our Bible, they certainly would have added the Apocrypha.

Bible Preservation & Translations
QUESTION #445

1.   How do we establish that the Greek and Hebrew words underlying the KJV are indeed the preserved words of God as promised in Psalms 12?

2.   What rules can be used to test the Hebrew and Greek manuscripts we have, to see if they are indeed the preserved words of God? Have these rules been used to successfully arrive at the TR and if so, where can we read this record?

3.   How much of the English translations prior to the AV1611 did the translators use for the end product? Can this be proved? Is it necessary to do so?

4.   I was told 80% of Tyndale's translation was used by the King James by a colleague who is not a scholar on the subject. Is this true?

5.   Was the Septuagint used as a source document for the KJV translation? If not, can it be proved. If so, is the Septuagint compatible with the TR?

6.   Was the Latin Vulgate ever used as part of the AV1611 translation? If not, can it be proved.

ANSWER #445

1.   God promised here to preserve His Hebrew Words in this Psalm. By extension, we include the Greek Words as well. For the preservation of the Words of the New Testament, Matthew 24:35; Mark 13:31; Luke 21:33; and Matthew 5:18 speak to this clearly. In the quotations of our Saviour from the O.T., He never questioned the Old Testament's accurate Words. If the Words were preserved for over 1500 years from Moses to Christ, why could they not be preserved for the next 1500 years until the printing press of John Gutenberg? Hence, we stand for the historic Masoretic Hebrew, Aramaic, and Greek Words. Of the total number of 5,255 Greek MSS in 1967, there are over 5,210

which stand with the Words underlying the KJB. <u>This is in addition to evidences from early versions and quotes from the early church fathers. So we accept Beza's 5th edition of 1598 as the most accurate copy of these preserved New Testament Greek Words.</u>

2.   Dean Burgon's five re-printed books by our Dean Burgon Society (DBS) are very helpful in this regard. He has eight "*tests of truth*'" for the Greek MSS. For O.T. the answer above is about the best that I know of. These conclusions must be based upon facts and also faith that God promised to preserve His Words and that He has fulfilled that promise. If so, which documents are preserved. See Matthew 24:35; Mark 13:31; Luke 21:33, and Matthew 5:18 for the Greek New Testament and the Old Testament Words being preserved.

3.   They probably used Tyndale and Bishop's Bible, but, most importantly, they compared everything with the originals.

4.   I understood they used over 95% or so. The only way to check this is to read both and compare.

5.   <u>The Septuagint (LXX) was not used for the KJB because it did not come into existence until the 200's A.D. as Origen's Hexapla.</u> Though there were a few O.T. books translated B.C. from Hebrew to Greek, the entire 39 books cannot be proved to be B.C.

6.   Dr. Edward Hills states that only 6 or 7 places were based on the Vulgate where the Greek MSS were not as full. 1 John 5:7-8 was one passage where the Latin had hundreds of MSS where the Greek only had 10 or so. See Edward Hills' *King James Bible Defended* for his position on this.

The Deity Of Christ

QUESTION #446

Is the meaning of the word "*Christ*" (defined as "*anointed One*"), by itself, enough to say that Jesus is God?

ANSWER #446

CHRISTOS means "*the anointed One*." The Hebrew, MASHIYACH, (which also means "*the anointed One*" which refers to the MESSIAH), is definitely DEITY. This is why the woman at the well and others wonder if He were "*the Christ*"--the fulfillment of prophecy. However, there are many other references to the Deity of the Lord Jesus Christ. These should all be used, not only the fact that He is "*the Christ*" of God.

Hebrews 1:8--Christ Is Called God
QUESTION #447

I must ask one more question with regard to Hebrews 1:8. Would you say that Lord God the Father is indeed talking to Jesus, calling him God? I believe, if I am correct, that this is possibly one of the most definitive verses that I have found for the argument of the Lord Jesus Christ as being a part of the Godhead.

ANSWER #447

God the Father is indeed talking to God the Son and calling Him "*God.*" His Deity is clear here. Bishop Westcott, however, in his book on Hebrews translates it something like this: "*God is Thy throne*" which completely nullifies His deity. Westcott did not believe in the Deity of Christ and mistranslated this verse to go along with this heresy.

The Omnipresence Of Christ
QUESTION #448

I heard teaching this morning suggesting the Lord Jesus may have permanently given up His ability to be omnipresent because he took on a human (albeit now glorified) body. Are there Scriptures that disprove this thinking?

ANSWER #448

The Lord Jesus Christ did not give up any of His Divine attributes when He took upon Himself a perfect human nature.

I spoke of this in my a.m. message.

Here are a few verses on His omniscience.

John 2:25 "*And needed not that any should testify of man: for he knew what was in man.*"

John 4:16-19 "*Jesus saith unto her, Go, call thy husband, and come hither. The woman answered and said, I have no husband. Jesus said unto her, Thou hast well said, I have no husband: For thou hast had five husbands; and he whom thou now hast is not thy husband: in that saidst thou truly. The woman saith unto him, Sir, I perceive that thou art a prophet.*"

John 4:29 "*Come, see a man, which told me all things that ever I did: is not this the Christ?*"

John 1:48 "*Nathanael saith unto him, Whence knowest thou me? Jesus answered and said unto him, Before that Philip called thee, when thou wast under the fig tree, I saw thee.*"

Omniscience Versus Omnipresence

QUESTION #449

Does "*omniscience*" have the same meaning as, or similar to, "*omnipresence*"?

ANSWER #449

"*Omniscience*" is "*all-knowing*." "*Omnipresence*" is "*everywhere present.*" These two attributes of the Lord are separate and distinct, though certainly they are interwoven because they are both attributes of Deity.

What Is Dispensationalism?

QUESTION #450

What is Dispensationalism? What does C. I. Scofield have to do with it?

ANSWER #450

I have several messages on dispensationalism. It is a method of properly understanding the Bible by rightly dividing it into the different ways God has dealt with human beings. The three largest dispensations are law, grace, and kingdom. The other four are usually innocence, conscience, human government, and promise. Dr. C. I. Scofield believed in dispensationalism and put it in his study Bible. I believe in all seven of these dispensations. It is the best way to understand the Bible properly from Genesis through Revelation.

The Two Natures Of The Saved

QUESTION #451

I have been struggling with assurance of salvation for two years now. I just find it very hard and lonely some times. I know that I am just to trust the finished work of Christ on the cross, and believe. But what about sin and not sharing the gospel and not reading the Bible enough? I struggle with all these things. I guess I can say like the apostle Paul, the evil that I do I do not want to do, and the good that I want to do I do not do, and the will to do good is there but I know not how. Who will deliver me from this body of death?

I also noticed in one of your comments on carnal Christians that you refer to Galatians 5:19-21:

> "*Now the works of the flesh are manifest, which are these; Adultery, fornication, uncleanness, lasciviousness, Idolatry, witchcraft, hatred, variance, emulations, wrath, strife, seditions, heresies, Envyings, murders, drunkenness, revellings, and such like: of the which I tell you before, as I have also told you in time past, that they which do such things shall not inherit the kingdom of God.*"

ANSWER #451

You must realize that if you are saved, you have two natures, the flesh and the Spirit. The nature you feed the most will win out in the struggle. The key verse is Galatians 5:16:

"This I say then, Walk in the Spirit, and ye shall not fulfil the lust of the flesh."

Without this walk, you will continue to walk in your flesh with all its doubts.

False Bible Preservation Position

QUESTION #452

What is your opinion on this statement? Here is the college text position statement that you requested:

"We believe that God has preserved His Word for every age. We accept the preservation of the Old Testament through the Hebrew Masoretic text; and we accept the preservation of the New Testament through the time-honored Byzantine, majority text stream represented by the Textus Receptus. We desire to teach the doctrines of inspiration and preservation in a faith-based, non-divisive manner. We use only the King James Version in our public ministry and academic work."

ANSWER #452

This sounds sound on the surface, at least. Here are a few of my comments.

1. "*Preserved His Word*" is the phrase used by the critical text Fundamentalists at Bob Jones University, Detroit Baptist Seminary, Calvary Baptist Seminary, Central Baptist Seminary and others, meaning by "*Word*" not "*Words*" but only "*thoughts, concepts, message, and ideas, but not Words*." In this context, it would be much clearer to reject or accept the re-definition of the "*Word of God*" which does not mean the Hebrew, Aramaic, and Greek "*Words*" of God.

I have answered Michael Sproul's book entitled "*GOD'S WORD PRESERVED*" where he fails to define that he means "*Words*." I call it "*A Critical Answer To Michael Sproul's God's Word Preserved--276 of Sproul's Statements Analyzed Carefully for Errors, Misrepresentations, and Serious Falsehoods*." I could send this to you if you're interested. As you know, he is in Tempe, AZ and, though he is a Majority Text man, he is in the BJU orbit regarding Bible Preservation of "*Word*" only and not "*Words*."

2. It would help to define which "*Hebrew Masoretic text*" should be used.

It would help to define it by saying the Hebrew and Aramaic Words underlying the KJB (if that is what is meant) since there are various "*Hebrew Masoretic texts*" floating around, some of these texts have changed the Hebrew Words by the Dead Sea Scrolls, the Septuagint (LXX), the Latin Vulgate, and other things in various places in the Old Testament.

3. It would help to define which "*Textus Receptus*" text should be used. Since there are probably 10 or 15 more "*Textus Receptus*" editions (like Stephens, Erasmus, Complutensian Polyglot, Beza, Elzevir, Scrivener's, etc. with each of these having 4, 5, or 6 editions). It would help to define it by saying the Greek Words underlying the King James Bible (if that is what is meant) which would mean in over 99.9% of the cases, Beza's 5th edition, 1598.

4. This is not a clear statement of the extent of either inspiration or preservation. Do they believe in verbal, plenary, inspiration of the Hebrew, Aramaic, and Greek Words (VPI) as I do, or do they have a modified position on inspiration which many are now taking? Do they believe in verbal, plenary, preservation of the Hebrew, Aramaic, and Greek Words (VPP) as I do, or do they have a modified position in preservation which many are now taking?

5. Though it sounds noble to "*teach the doctrines of inspiration and preservation*" in a "*non-divisive manner,*" let me make this observation:

a.   If their view of these two doctrines is the modified position, using the modified definition of "*Word*" of God (mentioned above) versus "*Words*" of God, they will be able to blend "*in a non-divisive manner*" with the prevailing Fundamental schools such as Bob Jones University, Detroit Baptist Seminary, Calvary Baptist Seminary, Central Baptist Seminary, Northland Baptist Bible College, Maranatha Baptist College, International Baptist College and Seminary, and others.

b.   If, however, they take the VPI and VPP position mentioned above, there is no way in the world that they will escape the wrath of the above-mentioned schools and others, in which case there will not be a "*non-divisive manner*" that will be able to prevail.

This is a very esoteric subject which is understood by very few. These are a few of my thoughts on this statement which, on the surface appears sound, as I said above, but I really don't know what would appear if someone were to take out a shovel and do a little excavation below the surface and go down to the foundations and specific definitions in this very profound and important theological subject.

Are All Spiritual Gifts For Today?
QUESTION #453
Please list the spiritual gifts which are operating in the church today.
ANSWER #453
I think the following GIFTS (properly interpreted and understood) are in the church today:

1 Corinthians 12:4-11
"Now there are diversities of gifts, but the same Spirit. 5 And there are differences of administrations, but the same Lord. 6 And there are diversities of operations, but it is the same God which worketh all in all. 7 But the manifestation of the Spirit is given to every man to profit withal. 8 For to one is given by the Spirit the word of wisdom; to another the word of knowledge by the same Spirit; 9 To another faith by the same Spirit; to another the gifts of healing by the same Spirit; 10 To another the working of miracles; to another prophecy; to another discerning of spirits; to another divers kinds of tongues; to another the interpretation of tongues: 11 But all these worketh that one and the selfsame Spirit, dividing to every man severally as he will."

1 Corinthians 12:28-30
"And God hath set some in the church, first apostles, secondarily prophets, thirdly teachers, after that miracles, then gifts of healings, helps, governments, diversities of tongues. 29 Are all apostles? are all prophets? are all teachers? are all workers of miracles? 30 Have all the gifts of healing? do all speak with tongues? do all interpret?"

On the following list, some of these are permanent gifts and some are temporary gifts:

Ephesians 4:8-12
"Wherefore he saith, When he ascended up on high, he led captivity captive, and gave gifts unto men. 9 (Now that he ascended, what is it but that he also descended first into the lower parts of the earth? 10 He that descended is the same also that ascended up far above all heavens, that he might fill all things.) 11 And he gave some, apostles; **(TEMPORARY)** *and some, prophets* **(TEMPORARY)**; *and some, evangelists; and some, pastors and teachers; 12 For the perfecting of the saints, for the work of the ministry, for the edifying of the body of Christ."*

On the following list, the first is a temporary gift and the rest are permanent gifts.

Romans 12:6-8

"Having then gifts differing according to the grace that is given to us, whether prophecy, let us prophesy according to the proportion of faith; **(TEMPORARY)** *7 Or ministry, let us wait on our ministering: or he that teacheth, on teaching; 8 Or he that exhorteth, on exhortation: he that giveth, let him do it with simplicity; he that ruleth, with diligence; he that sheweth mercy, with cheerfulness."*

I believe the "*temporary gifts*" were apostolic gifts in effect before the Bible was completed in 90-100 A.D. After that, these gifts ceased.

1 Cor. 13:10's Meaning Of "Perfect"
QUESTION #454

I request you to explain the meaning of "*perfect*" in the phrase, "*when that which is perfect is come*" (1 Corinthians 13:10).

ANSWER #454

The word used here for "perfect" is TELEIOS. Here are the various meanings:

5046 teleios {tel'-I-os}

from 5056; TANT - 8:67,1161; adj

AV - perfect 17, man 1, of full age 1; 19

1) brought to its end, finished

2) wanting nothing necessary to completeness

3) perfect

4) that which is perfect

  4a) consummate human integrity and virtue

  4b) of men

   4b1) full grown, adult, of full age, mature

The word, TELEION, is in the neuter gender here. As such, I believe "*that which is perfect*" refers to the completion of the New Testament in 90 to 100 A.D. I believe that is when the so-called "*sign gifts*" of tongues and others ceased.

Dean Burgon Society & Inerrancy
QUESTION #455

Does the Dean Burgon Society (DBS) subscribe to biblical inerrancy in regards to translations or revisions? Or is biblical inerrancy limited only to the originals and accurate copies of the originals that we have today? Is there a possibility of error, be it scientific, or theological, (or whatever) in the KJB? If so, where? The question rises after speaking with a friend of mine who holds to biblical inerrancy in the originals, but not to any one version or revision, including the KJB.

ANSWER #455

The DBS puts inerrancy at the point of the original Hebrew, Aramaic, and Greek Words and accurate COPIES of those Words that we possess today.

Translations by MAN are as INERRANT as MAN is. We know MAN is NOT INERRANT, but is FALLIBLE and IMPERFECT. Only GOD is INERRANT and INFALLIBLE and PERFECT.

I never use the word "inerrant" or "infallible" for any translation in any language, whether English, Spanish, French, German, Chinese, Japanese, etc.

As to the KJB being inerrant, I don't use that term for the KJB. By not using "*inerrant*," I don't believe it is "*errant*." I just believe "*inerrant*" belongs to God Himself, not to man or anything man does. For instance, just look at the pitiful and disgraceful action they took in making the Apocrypha a part of their 1611 edition!! As you may know, the Apocrypha contradicts the Bible in many places. In the Apocrypha, lying is all right at times, suicide is all right, and other things. The KJB's from the beginning had all kinds of changes, corrections, printers errors, etc. I mention some of these in my book, *Defending the King James Bible* (**BFT #1594 @ $12.00 + $7.00 S&H**).

I prefer to use the term "*accurate*," "*true*," "*faithful*" and "*reliable*" for the King James Bible. I believe that the KJB is the only accurate translation in the English language. I don't think there are any "*translation errors*" in the KJB, but there were certainly printers errors like those in the Oxford edition versus the Cambridge edition such as in the following three errors in Oxford versus Cambridge.

All you have to do is to find just one tiny mistake, and inerrancy flies out the window. Only God Himself and His Words can be genuinely inerrant and infallible. We might try to approach these traits, but being sinful human beings, we can never attain to it.

THREE DIFFERENCES BETWEEN
OXFORD & CAMBRIDGE KING JAMES BIBLES:

By Pastor D. A. Waite, Th.D., Ph.D.

December 18, 1998

(1) **Jeremiah 34:16**, as found in AV 1611, Hebrew, and Cambridge KJB

"*But ye turned and polluted my name, and caused every man his servant, and every man his handmaid,* **whom _ye_ had set at liberty** *at their pleasure, to return, and brought them into subjection, to be unto you for servants and for handmaids. (KJV)"*

Found in error in the Oxford KJB & others "*whom __he__ had set at liberty*"

    (2) **2 Chronicles 33:19** as found in AV 1611, Hebrew, and Cambridge KJB

> "*His prayer also, and how God was increased of him,* **and all his sin**, *and his trespass, and the places wherein he built high places, and set up groves and graven images, before he was humbled: behold, they are written among the sayings of the seers.*"

Found in error in the Oxford KJB & others "*and all his __sins__*"

    (3) **Nahum 3:16** as found in AV 1611, Hebrew, and Cambridge KJB

> "*Thou hast multiplied thy merchants above the stars of heaven: the cankerworm spoileth,* **and _flieth_ away**."

Found in error in the Oxford KJB & others "*and __fleeth__ away*"

Demon-Possession Of Christians?

QUESTION #456

I am not a Pentecostal or charismatic. I am an independent Baptist. Recently, I met one of the Pentecostal pastors. He wants to cast away evil spirits.

I have another question. Can demons possess a believer?

ANSWER #456

I believe the Bible teaches that though a believer might be influenced by demons, he cannot be "*possessed*" by demons or the devil. 1 Corinthians 6:19-20 teaches clearly that the bodies of born-again Christians are the temples of God the Holy Spirit. Satan cannot "*possess*" what God the Holy Spirit has previously "*possessed.*"

Is Speaking In Tongues For Today?

QUESTION #457

Is speaking in tongues still a proper gift to be used in the church? Please list the spiritual gifts which are still operating in the church today.

ANSWER #457

I think the following gifts (properly interpreted and understood) are **not** in the church today:

1 Corinthians 12:4-11

"*Now there are diversities of gifts, but the same Spirit. 5 And there are differences of administrations, but the same Lord. 6 And there are diversities of operations, but it is the same God which worketh all in all. 7 But the manifestation of the Spirit is given to every man to profit withal. 8 For to one is given by the Spirit **the word of wisdom**; to another **the word of knowledge** by the same Spirit; 9 To another* [special kind of supernatural] ***faith** by the same Spirit; to another the **gifts of healing** by the same Spirit; 10 To another **the working of miracles**; to another **prophecy**; to another **discerning of spirits**; to another **divers kinds of tongues**; to another the **interpretation of tongues**: 11 But all these worketh that one and the selfsame Spirit, dividing to every man severally as he will.*"

1 Corinthians 12:28-30

Most of the following gifts are temporary. Two are permanent.

"*And God hath set some in the church, first **apostles**, secondarily **prophets**, thirdly **teachers** [permanent], after that **miracles**, then gifts of **healings, helps, governments**, [permanent] **diversities of tongues**. 29 Are all **apostles**? are all **prophets**? are all **teachers** [permanent]? are all **workers of miracles**? 30 Have all the **gifts of healing**? do all **speak with tongues**? do all **interpret**"?*

Some of the following gifts are temporary and some are permanent.

Ephesians 4:8-12

Two of the following gifts were temporary and two are permanent:

"*Wherefore he saith, When he ascended up on high, he led captivity captive, and gave gifts unto men. 9 (Now that he ascended, what is it but that he also descended first into the lower parts of the earth? 10 He that descended is the same also that ascended up far above all heavens, that he might fill all things.) 11 And he gave some, **apostles**; [temporary] and some, **prophets** [temporary]; and some, **evangelists**; and some, **pastors** and **teachers**; 12 For the perfecting of the saints, for the work of the ministry, for the edifying of the body of Christ:*"

I believe all but one of the following gifts are still with us today:

Romans 12:6-8

"*Having then gifts differing according to the grace that is given to us, whether **prophecy**, [temporary] let us prophesy according to the proportion of faith; 7 Or **ministry**, let us wait on our ministering: or he that **teacheth**, on teaching; 8 Or he that **exhorteth**, on exhortation: he that **giveth**, let him do it with simplicity; he that* *ruleth*, with diligence; he that **sheweth mercy**, with cheerfulness."

This is a big subject. If you are a Pentecostal or a charismatic, you will differ with me on this. I believe that many of these gifts were apostolic gifts which are no longer in the church after the Bible was completed in about 90-100 A.D.

"Perfect" In 1 Corinthians 13:10
QUESTION #458

Please give a brief explanation of the word, "*perfect*" in 1 Corinthians 13.10.

ANSWER #458

The word used for "*perfect*" with its various meanings is:
te,leioj teleios {tel'-i-os}

Meaning: 1) brought to its end, finished 2) **wanting nothing necessary to completeness** 3) perfect 4) that which is perfect 4a) consummate human integrity and virtue 4b) of men 4b1) full grown, adult, of full age, **mature**
Origin: from 5056; TANT - 8:67,1161; adj
Usage: AV - perfect 17, man 1, of full age 1; 19

The form or the word is in the neuter case here. As such, I believe "*that which is perfect*" refers to the completion of the New Testament which happened in about 90 to 100 A.D. I believe that is when the so-called "*sign gifts*" of tongues, and others, ceased.

Verbal Plenary Preservation (VPP)
QUESTION #459

What is your comment about Verbal Plenary Preservation(VPP)?

ANSWER #459

I believe that the Bible promises the verbal, plenary preservation of the original Hebrew, Aramaic, and Greek Words of the Bible. I believe this promise has been fulfilled in the Traditional Hebrew, Aramaic, and Greek Words underlying the King James Bible.

The N.T. Canon And Jude
QUESTION #460

I came across a commentary about the Book of Jude. It said that the Book of Jude was not added to Canon until the 4th Century Church. Is that true? If so, why would there be controversy about whether it was to be part of Canon or not?

ANSWER #460

I do not know the details of the date when Jude was put into the Canon, but I would imagine it would be around the same time as the others which was at the Council of Nicea of about 325 A.D.

Dave Hunt Denies Literal Hell Fire

QUESTION #461

Here are some quotes by Dave Hunt on literal "*fire*" in Hell. What do you think of his position? Is it Biblical?

> "*As for why I don't believe the flames of hell are physical*, I have given many sound biblical reasons for that conviction."

> "*It is astonishing to me that anyone would imagine that in order for the flames of hell to be "real" they must be physical.*"

> "*The rich man in hell was "tormented in this flame." He begged Abraham to send Lazarus to "dip the tip of his finger in water, and cool my tongue..." (Luke 16:23-24 [2]). Were the flames in hell and the thirst that tormented the rich man real? Certainly. Were they physical? How could that be the case*?"

> "*Another brother repeatedly refers to physical flames and physical fire as essential if the fires of hell are "real.*"

> "*I have given many reasons why the flames in the lake of fire, though real, could not be physical:*"

> "*No physical body could survive the lake of fire for a moment*. It would instantly be consumed -- so God would have to continually, moment by moment, reconstitute the physical bodies so He could continue to torment the damned."

> "*Why would God choose to use physical fire to torment the damned* even though it didn't consume them? Shouldn't they instead be tormented by the flaming fire of an overwhelming sense of the exceeding sinfulness of the sins they have committed (Romans 7:13 [9]) and the horror of what it means to rebel against the only true God, Creator of heaven and earth? *Wouldn't this burning of the conscience be far worse than burning in physical flames*?"

ANSWER #461

Thanks for the various quotes from Dave Hunt, some of which I have included above.

He freely admits that the fires of Hell are not literal fires. He spiritualizes what should not be spiritualized. Remember what has been called "The Golden Rule of Bible Interpretation":

"When the plain sense of the Bible makes plain sense, seek no other sense. Therefore, take every word at its primary, ordinary, usual, literal meaning, unless the facts of the immediate context, studied in the light of related passages, and axiomatic and fundamental truths, indicate clearly otherwise. God, in revealing His Word, neither intends nor permits the reader to be confused. He wants His children to understand." (Author Unknown)

In these various quotes, Dave Hunt is giving an apostate position on the fire of Hell, clear and simple. Bible-believing Christians should approach his teachings with great caution. He is mistaken on this subject of literal fire in Hell. He is mistaken on the blood of Christ, defending John MacArthur's heretical position that the blood of Christ is not literal, but only a metonym or figure of speech for death. He is mistaken for having his main assistant a man who hates the Textus Receptus and the King James Bible but believes, rather, in the Gnostic Critical Greek Text. If you read Dave Hunt's material, beware of these and perhaps other clear errors as well.

Meaning Of "Departure"
QUESTION #462

In trying to define "*departures*," can it be construed as a "*departure*" the rendering of a word or phrase that weakens Christian doctrine? Could the example of using "*pit*" or "*sepulcher*" an example of "*departure*," if the Hebrew has "*sheol*" and the KJB translators translated it "*Hell*"?

ANSWER #462

Some of the definitions of "DEPARTURE" are as follows:

departure

noun

1 a departing, or going away
2 a starting out, as on a trip or new course of action
3 a deviation or turning aside (from)
4 [Archaic] death
5 Naut. the distance due east or west from the meridian of its starting point covered by a ship on a given course

Etymology

[ME derived from OFr departeure]

Yes, I believe "*pit*" weakens "*sheol*" for "*Hell*." Here are the various meanings of SHEOL in Hebrew: You notice that even the KJB used "*pit*" three times for "*sheol*" and 31 times for "*grave*" and 31 times for "*Hell*." Depending on the context, it might be a weakening in places where it should be translated "*Hell*." But in some cases, perhaps, as the KJB did, you could make it "*grave*" or "*pit*" if the context is clear. But never to use "*Hell*" for "*sheol*" certainly would be a definite weakening and departure in my judgment.

Here are some of the meanings of SHEOL:
from 07592; TWOT - 2303c; n f
   AV - grave 31, hell 31, pit 3; 65
   1) sheol, underworld, grave, hell, pit
     1a) the underworld
     1b) Sheol - the OT designation for the abode of the dead
       1b1) place of no return
       1b2) without praise of God
       1b3) wicked sent there for punishment
       1b4) righteous not abandoned to it
       1b5) of the place of exile (fig)
       1b6) of extreme degradation in sin

Where the context is clear, using "hades" for the Greek word, "hades" (which is a mere transliteration) rather than translating it as "Hell" is also a departure. These are departures in translation. There are many other departures because of wrong Words that underlie a given translation.

Biblical Creation In Genesis 1

QUESTION #463

A friend and I have received an email from someone who is trying to "*correct the Bible*" from the Hebrew in Genesis 1. Supposedly he knows Hebrew. The two things he's saying are as follows:

1. The days of creation don't have a definite article before them.

2. "*The heaven*" should be plural in verse 1. Do you cover that in any of your books, or could you recommend someone else I could call or read something from about it?

Thank you for your time, and praise the Lord for your ministry! I've read some articles of yours, and I heard a debate between you and James White, and greatly appreciate your sober and mature representation of the Received Text/KJB position.

ANSWER #463

Here are a few comments about both of these questions you have asked:

1. The article is not needed when you have the words, "*first*," "*second*," and so on. These words themselves make the days definite. Furthermore, the specific words "*the evening and the morning*" make clear that it is a solar day.

2. Sometimes Hebrew plurals can be taken in a collective sense. When

this is the case, the plural word can be translated as a singular. Another example of this is found also in Genesis 1:1. In the phrase, "*God created*," the word for "*God*" (ELOHIM) is a Hebrew plural signifying three or more. Yet we do not translate it as a plural, "*Gods*." Does he also say the King James Bible should have translated it "GODS"? I wouldn't bother with this man's criticisms. Go right on standing for the KJB and its underlying Hebrew, Aramaic, and Greek Words.

Is There Biblical Mathematics?
QUESTION #464
Do you have access to any mathematics to show that the Bible is accurate? I know it's accurate but I want to show it to an atheist.

ANSWER #464
I don't have such information. I don't believe that God uses this mathematics method to show His Words are accurate.

Meaning Of "Saved In Childbearing"
QUESTION #465
I am so thankful for your helping me in my Bible study. I have another difficult verse which is 1 Timothy 2:15: "*Notwithstanding she shall be saved in childbearing, if they continue in faith and charity and holiness with sobriety.*"

What does it really mean? I need your help. May God bless you in His service.

ANSWER #465
I believe it is referring to Eve's bearing of her son, Seth, to continue the line that would one day be that of the Messiah, the Lord Jesus Christ. By her "*childbearing*" and in the coming of the Lord Jesus Christ, those who genuinely trust and receive Him will be "*saved.*"

The Bible's Meaning Of "Adoption"
QUESTION #466
Pastor do you have a teaching that will help a man that has just been saved to understand what it means that God has now adopted him as a son. We do not want him to start thinking he is the same as Christ, but to share that the Father loves him.

ANSWER #466

Have the man look at the 5 verses on "*adoption*" (Romans 8:15, 8:23; 9:4, Galatians 4:5, and Ephesians 1:5. John 1:12 shows that by genuine faith we can become "*sons of God.*" This is God's adoption method. It does not equate us with the Lord Jesus Christ, however. He was the Son of God as Deity.

The Kingdom of God "Within"?
QUESTION #467
I am reading through Scofield's Bible this year. I came across two footnotes that I am not sure about. Could you comment on them? The passages are: Luke 17.21--"*The kingdom of God is within you.*" and Luke 18.8--"*shall he find faith on the earth?*"

ANSWER #467
1. Luke 17:21 The word, "*within*" can be understood as "*among you*" because the Lord Jesus Christ was there in His Person. Since the "*kingdom of God*" has to do with being born-again. In that sense, it is truly "*within*" those who are saved.

1787 **entos** {en-tos'}

from 1722; prep

AV - within 2; 2

1) within, inside

  1a) within you i.e. **in the midst of you**

  1b) within you i.e. your soul

Another sense could be taken as well. It could refer to the "*kingdom*" of the Lord Jesus Christ "*in the midst*" of them because if they had accepted Him, the Millennium could have begun.

2. Luke 18:8, "*faith*" has the article with it, "*the faith*" which means the New Testament body of doctrine and teachings. Apostasy will be so rampant when the Lord Jesus Christ will return in the rapture of the saved ones that "*the faith*" will be very scarce or even nonexistent.

Jesus Christ's "*Prepared Body*"
QUESTION #468
I was just wondering where in the Bible does it tell us Christ was given a "*body prepared*" for Him by God for His birth?

ANSWER #468
I believe Hebrews 10:5 is the verse you want. It is an account of when the Lord Jesus Christ came into the world at His incarnation. He prayed to God the Father:

Hebrews 10:5 "*Wherefore when He cometh into the world, He saith,*

Sacrifice and offering thou wouldest not, but a body hast Thou prepared Me:"

In my opinion, that "*body*" prepared by God the Father included every part of the Lord Jesus Christ's body, His hands, His feet, His blood, His nerves, His skin, His hair, and every other part of His body.

Two Creations, Or Only One?
QUESTION #469

We have questions that we feel only you can answer for us. The book, *Ezekiel*, written by Gerald Flurry mentions Genesis 1:2, stating that "*God never wants to risk having another 'tohu and bohu,' a wasted and desolate Earth.*" We do not understand what "*tohu and bohu*" mean, also have been informed by "*experts*" that God had two creations. We cannot find this in our King James Bible. When you have time, we would appreciate your view on this. Thank you.

ANSWER #469

Genesis 1:2 "*And the earth was **without form, and void**; and darkness was upon the face of the deep. And the Spirit of God moved upon the face of the waters.*"

Jeremiah 4:23 "*I beheld the earth, and, lo, it was **without form, and void**; and the heavens, and they had no light.*"

These two verses both have "*without form and void*" which is the translation of the Hebrew "*tohu and bohu.*" This was the state of the earth before God created the creatures in the sea, in the air, and on the land including man.

I disagree completely with Mr. Flurry's view of "*two creations*." There was no pre-Adamic civilization as some Bible teachers have taught like Clarence Larkin and others.

The verse that closes all argument is found in 1 Corinthians 15:45:
"*And so it is written, The **first man Adam** was made a living soul; the last Adam was made a quickening spirit.*"
Genesis tells of the only creation of man (Adam) and the New Testament clearly teaches that Adam was the "*first man.*" That settles it for me.

Bible Preservation Explained Briefly
QUESTION #470

What would be your recommendation for a short introduction on the subject of Bible preservation?

ANSWER #470

I believe a simple and short introduction to Bible Preservation is found in Chapter I of my book, *Defending the King James Bible* (BFT #1594 @ **$12.00 + $7.00 S&H**).

My Position Is Not Peter Ruckman's
QUESTION #471

I have just been listening to your radio talk given in 2006, No. #1 of Sproul's Anti-KJV book, and it raises a few questions for me.

Regarding today's radio talk, Michael Sproul says (acc. to your points 35-38, approx.) there's hardly any difference between your approach to the Greek TR text, and Peter Ruckman's position. I realize that's an overstatement, but the difficulty comes with trying to determine whether the KJV translators were protected from error, when they chose the Beza text (1598) over Erasmus, (1514) or over Stephanus (1550).

ANSWER #471

I am totally opposed to the position of Peter Ruckman who teaches falsely that the KJB was verbally inspired by God and therefore can correct the Hebrew, Aramaic, and Greek Words from which it was taken. He puts the inspired, inerrant, infallible and perfect terms in referring to the English KJB rather than the Hebrew, Aramaic, and Greek Words that underlie it.. I believe this to be heresy. I place all of these terms on the underlying Hebrew, Aramaic, and Greek Words rather than on the KJB. These two views are 100% different. I would hope you could see these two positions clearly.

I also deny perfection for the KJB translators. They were just imperfect, fallen men like the rest of humanity. However, I believe they gave us the only accurate translation of the proper Hebrew, Aramaic, and Greek Words in the English language to date. You can differ with my view if you wish, but that is my position on the KJB. I develop my belief on this in my book, *Defending the King James Bible* (BFT #1594 @ $12.00 + $7.00) which you perhaps have read.

You don't have to agree with me that the Hebrew, Aramaic, and Greek Words underlying the KJB are the preserved original Words and are therefore inspired, inerrant, infallible, and perfect. These Words must be the basis for every translation in the world.

For the New Testament, this would be Scrivener's Greek text which is 99% Beza's 5th edition, 1598. That is my standard though I cannot prove it to anyone. I believe it by facts and faith. You can have any standard you wish, but that is mine. I am not interested in debating with Robert Martin or you, or anyone else on this matter. I believe it is a waste of time. I have many more important things to do with my time. "*A man convinced against his will is of the same opinion still*." as the old saying goes.

What Is The "Gospel"?

QUESTION #472

You have confused me about the gospel. How can it have so many definitions? I don't see this in Scripture.

ANSWER #472

I'm sorry that you are confused about the gospel.

Here is what I try to say about making the "*gospel*" clear as I preach the gospel. I believe there are two phases: defining the gospel, and then clearly preaching the "*gospel*."

The "*gospel*" is defined as the good news about what the Lord Jesus Christ did for all the sinners of the world. Clearly preaching the "*gospel*" (or evangelizing) consists of three parts:

(1) a person must "*repent*" (METANOIA "*change his mind*") about his sin. He must realize that God calls him a sinner, that he is a sinner, and that he cannot pay for those sins himself.

(2) Secondly, a person must change his mind about the Saviour. He must realize that the Lord Jesus Christ is the Son of God Who shed His blood on the cross in order to successfully bear the sins of the world.

(3) In the third place, he must genuinely receive and trust the Lord Jesus Christ as his Saviour by personal faith in Him.

"Holy Ghost" And "Holy Spirit"

QUESTION #473

Is there anyone there who can tell me what seems to be the principle that the King James translators used when translating the Greek word PNEUMA ("*Spirit*") as it applies to the terms Spirit, Holy Spirit, and Holy Ghost. Do we know why they chose to use the term Holy Ghost in some instances and Holy Spirit in other instances to translate the Greek word PNEUMA?

ANSWER #473

I don't know for certain any "*principle*" involved. Some have said that "*Ghost*" was used when mentioned as a part of the Trinity. "*Holy Ghost*" is used **89 times** in the King James Bible. It is used only in the New Testament. "*Holy Spirit*" is used only **7 times** in the King James Bible, three in the Old Testament and four in the New Testament. "Spirit" was used at other times. Sorry for no more help on this. In 1611, "*ghost*" and "*spirit*" had nearly identical meanings. There was not the problem at that time as we have now with the various meanings of the word, "*ghost*."

Calvinist, Arminian, Or What?
QUESTION #474

Are you a Calvinist or Arminian? I have seen a quote from your book *Defending the King James Bible* which seems to defend Calvinism.

ANSWER #474

I am a Biblicist, not a strict Calvinist nor a strict Arminian. I believe whatever the Bible teaches on every doctrine that is contained therein. I do not follow the philosophies of men such as John Calvin or Jacobus Arminius.

I am totally opposed to hyper-Calvinism that teaches that Christ died only for the elect. He died for the sins of the whole world. John 3:16 (and many other verses) makes this clear.

The New Heaven And New Earth
QUESTION #475

I have a question to ask you. In Revelation, where God talks about a new heaven and a new earth, does that happen after the tribulation and at the beginning of the 1,000 year millennial kingdom, or does it occur after the thousand year reign of the Lord Jesus Christ?

ANSWER #475

Since this phrase comes in Revelation 21, it appears that the new heaven and the new earth will be created after the 1,000 year millennial reign of the Lord Jesus Christ. Other verses that use "*new heavens*" are Isaiah 65:17, 66:22, and 2 Peter 3:13.

Who Is "Allah"?

QUESTION #476

What do you think about an article about the word, "Allah"?

ANSWER #476

Here are a few comments on this Muslim article by Rick Brown:

1.   I'm not certain about the Moon God situation, but I neither accept it or reject it at present. This is not the chief objection I have to the article, however.#495

2.   Brown's bibliology is flawed where he refers to the Bible writers as being "*inspired authors.*"

First, they were not "*inspired,*" their "Words" were "*inspired.*"

Second, they were not "*authors*" but only the "*writers.*" God is the "*Author.*" This is found in the first column of page 21.8 in the article (8/10ths down the page).

3.   I dispute his statement that: "*the word Allah has no other meaning in Arabic than the one true God, . . .*" This is totally false. The one true God is a Trinity. Allah despises our Triune God and denies the Deity of the Lord Jesus Christ. This is found in the second column, page 21.2.

4.   I dispute his quote that "*Muslims, Jews, and Christians believe in the same God.*" This is found in the second column, page 21.9. We have a Triune God, Muslims and Jews reject Him.

5.   I dispute his similar statements on the first column of pages 22.1, 22.4, and 22.9.

6.   For him, anyone's "*god*" is the same as our "*God*" which is an apostate view of our God. Does he have the same view of all of the tens of thousands of heathen "*gods*" including the totem poles and the buddhas in the world?

7.   He does better in the conclusion where he says: "*Nevertheless, their concept of God is incomplete and distorted without the revelation of God that is presented in the Bible.*" This is found in the second column, p. 25.6.

Is Salvation A "Process"

QUESTION #477

I post in a Christian forum and there is a person who always claims that salvation comes through following Jesus and living sinless. She says it is a process. To me this sounds heretical, but at the same time there are also verses in the Bible which confuse me and make me ask myself whether salvation might not also somehow depend on living holier and making progress. For example today I read Galatians 5:19-24 and there Paul lists all kinds of sins and says that those who do them will not enter the kingdom of God. Later, Paul says that Christians have crucified the flesh together with all their desires. Does this mean that a Christian cannot or must not have any of these sins which are listed in Galatians 5:19?

Actually a lot of preachers say this. According to them you cannot be a Christian and have any problems with big sin only with small sins. But what if you have problems with things such as anger? What do you do then? Does this mean that you cannot be a Christian and have any problems with this? When I read verses like these then I feel condemned, because I'm aware of those problems, but at the same time I don't really know how to change them.

ANSWER #477

John 5:24 makes it clear that when we're saved, we pass "*from death unto life*" at that very instant. Redemption is not a "*process*." It is an instantaneous transformation. The false versions of 1 Peter 2:2 say "*so that by it you may grow into salvation* " (New Revised Standard Version) which implies a "*process*."

As far as salvation depending on our living, you must remember that Romans 7:18 says clearly that "*in me, that is my flesh dwelleth no good thing*." Our old natures are evil and not good. The new nature of God the Holy Spirit Who lives within the redeemed people, must win the battle with the flesh.

The Source Of The Trinity
QUESTION #478

I believe that the KJV translators were influenced by their Anglican/Catholic belief system. God existing as "*three Persons in One*" is a Catholic doctrinal position gleaned from the Babylonian Mysteries. Do you agree?

ANSWER #478

I deny that "*God existing as three Persons in One*" (the Trinity) originated from the "*Catholic doctrinal position*" that came from "*Babylonian Mysteries*." It came straight from the Bible. I disagree on this important doctrinal point.

Polytheism And The Trinity
QUESTION #479

Only two or three Scriptures in the KJV are used as "proof" texts to support "*polytheism*" which was passed along to the Protestant Church through the Reformation. On the other hand, the preponderance of scriptures in the KJV support monotheism, for examples, "*The Lord our God is one Lord,*" and Jesus' words "*I and my Father are one.*" The Father and the Son have many titles, some distinct, and some shared. Just as *"Son of God"* and *"Son of man"* refer to the same being, so does *"God the Father"* and *"God the Holy Ghost"* refer to the same Being.

ANSWER #479

The New Testament does not teach *"polytheism"* as you say. I do not believe that Trinitarianism is *"polytheism."* Trinitarianism is the belief in one God in three separate and distinct Persons. You are totally in error when you say that "*'God the Father' and 'God the Holy Ghost' refer to the same Being."* They are distinct Persons in the Godhead and are not to be confused as you have confused Them. I believe your position on the Trinity to be unscriptural and also a very serious heresy.

The 10 Commandments & The N.T.

QUESTION #480

You may be able to answer a query I have had for some time. Why do Baptists ignore the 10 commandments? I have always believed that Baptists were God-loving Christians, but this question has been constantly bothering me.

ANSWER #480

I am a dispensational Baptist who is not under any part of the three divisions of the law of Moses. Only 9 of the 10 commandments are repeated in the New Testament, therefore I do not *"ignore"* them, but seek to obey them. Keeping the Saturday Sabbath, however, is not repeated, and therefore should not be obeyed in our New Testament age. We worship our Saviour on the first day of the week which was the day of His bodily resurrection.

Belief In Christ Is A "Choice"

QUESTION #481

Since we are responsible for believing on, or rejecting Jesus, can a Christian boast that He is saved because He chose to believe, whereas the unbeliever made the wrong choice? I am trying to understand the doctrines of election and free will.

Six months ago I used to believe TULIP was biblical. I discovered your website through SermonAudio.com. I feel blessed by your teachings on dispensationalism.

ANSWER #481

I'm glad you like our website. We should be careful about boasting, but it is true that those of us who are saved are saved by our genuine faith in and trust in the Lord Jesus Christ as our Saviour. By the same token, those who are lost, are lost because they have not personally trusted in the Lord Jesus Christ as their Saviour who died for their sins. Choice is involved in salvation. Accepting or rejecting the Lord Jesus Christ as Saviour is God's measure of who goes to Heaven and who goes to Hell.

"Spiritual Warfare"

QUESTION #482

There has been something I have wanted to ask you about your thoughts on spiritual warfare and disease. Could this be something of an attack in the form of disease? I don't know if that can be substantiated biblically or not.

ANSWER #482

As far as your question on *"spiritual warfare,"* let me say this. I know some people who stress this. I have shied away from it. From the way some people write and talk about it, I wonder if it is a cult or an offshoot of the charismatic movement. I know from Ephesians we *"wrestle not against flesh and blood"* (Eph. 6:12a), but the Lord has not laid out the methods of this warfare other than the spiritual *"armour"* (Ephesians 6:13a) including *"praying always"* (Ephesians 6:18).

Am I A "Calvinist" Or What?

QUESTION #483

You are not Calvinist are you? I am not at all. However, I do believe the Lord calls certain Christians to do certain things. I know I should be:

"ready always to give an answer to every man that asketh you a reason of the hope that is in you with meekness and fear:"

ANSWER #483

No, I am not a *"Calvinist."* I believe the Bible is clear that *"whosoever will, let him take the water of life freely"* (Revelation 22:17b). Many other verses make it clear that the Lord Jesus Christ died for the sins of the world, not just for the "elect." John 3:16 is clear that God the Father loved the entire "world" and sent His Son so that *"**whosoever** believeth in Him* [**not just the 'elect'**] *should not perish, but have everlasting life."*

If you have a fast Internet, you can go to our website (BibleForToday.org) and watch our services on Sundays at 10 a.m. and 1:30 p.m. (Eastern) and on Thursdays at 8 p.m. (Eastern) on the BROWN BOX.

Are Fallen Angels In Genesis 6?
QUESTION #484

Do you have any info or a sermon regarding this matter? Some say fallen angels had offspring with human women. Some say the sons of God were men rejected by God. Any help would greatly be appreciated.

ANSWER #484

I believe these "*giants*" were "*fallen ones*" (NEPHILIM) who were the product of fallen angels and human women. Because these creatures would pollute the human race and make it impossible to have a perfect and pure human being, the Lord Jesus Christ, God had to judge by death that entire population and spare only eight people who were willing to enter into Noah's ark during the universal flood. By this means, God preserved a pure human seed line untainted by these "*fallen ones*" (NEPHILIM) who had corrupted the human race.

Understanding "Bible Preservation"
QUESTION #485

Would you subscribe to the copied position (quoted below) on the preservation of the Words of God? I don't. I believe the Words of God are preserved in the Textus Receptus of which the KJV is a faithful translation. The following quote is from a church. There is no mention of the Hebrew, Aramaic, or Greek Words. This is their sum total of their position:

> "*By the 'Holy Bible' we mean that collection of sixty-six books from Genesis to The Revelation, divinely preserved in the English language and commonly known as the authorized, King James Version of 1611 A.D.*"

This position is not good. Not even the KJV translators felt this way about their production. I find this position among many of my contemporaries in the independent Baptist group of churches. I believe it is a cop-out position so as not to have to defend one's position on just how God has preserved His Words. It is easier just to say the KJV is the divinely preserved Word of God and not have to understand or defend the position. I fear that we (all within the independent Baptist group) will be seen as non-thinkers and become powerless to present to this world an authoritative position upon the Words of God. I think there is still much confusion abounding concerning the preservation of God's Words. I appreciate your stand and hope and pray that God will continue to give you strength and grace to counsel, teach, encourage and defend a good position concerning God's Words.

ANSWER #485

We must keep capital "P" Preservation at the point of the Hebrew, Aramaic, and Greek Words underlying the King James Bible. Sometimes I use the small "p" "preservation" for the KJB insofar as it "*preserves*" in English the accurate translation of the proper Hebrew, Aramaic, and Greek Words that underlie it. I agree with you that it is an error to make capital "P" Preservation for any translation, the KJB included. That is the position of Peter Ruckman, Gail Riplinger, and their followers. It is not supported by the Bible.

God never promised to Preserve His Words in any translation, only in His original Hebrew, Aramaic, and Greek Words. I believe He has done so in those preserved original Words that underlie our KJB. As you know, the subtitle of my *Defending the King James Bible* book (**BFT #1594 @ $12.00 + $7.00 S&H**) is "*God's Words Kept Intact In English*." I think this is a good way to phrase it.

CHAPTER III
QUESTIONS ABOUT
NEW TESTAMENT
WORD MEANINGS

The Meaning Of "Sometimes"
QUESTION #486

As you know, I use the King James Bible and it is my Bible of preference. With your *Defined King James Bible*, the Old English wasn't a problem and I've really grown in the Word much more since switching to the King James Bible. However, over time, I have found the word, "*sometimes*," that is used in the King James Bible, can be confusing. It is in today's reading in Ephesians 5:8. Something must have happened to the word ,"*sometimes*," from the Old English to our modern day English. In the footnotes it mentions that "*sometimes*" actually means once, formerly which is quite different from "*sometimes*" and its meaning today. I would actually much rather read those verses that have "*sometimes*" in the Old English with the word "*formerly*." If I memorized that verse, I'd feel like I had to memorize it with "*sometimes*" because that is the way it is in the Old English, when I'd much rather memorize it with use of the word "*formerly*" but then I'd feel like I was being disloyal to the cause.

ANSWER #486

The word used for "*sometimes*" in Ephesians 5:8 is POTE. It has various meanings such as:

4218 <u>pote</u> {pot-eh'}

from the base of 4225 and 5037; particle

AV - in time past 5, at any time 4, in times past 3, sometimes 3,
    sometime 3, once 2, not tr 3, misc 9; 32

1) once i.e. <u>formerly</u>, aforetime, at some time

As you can see, it is translated "*sometimes*" only 3 times out of 32. You can read it as it appears, and explain it any way you wish.

Meaning Of 2 Thessalonians 2:2
QUESTION #487

Should the word in 2 Thessalonians 2:2 be day of "*Christ*" or day of the "*Lord*" as Scofield states? It is interesting in his old edition he states there are several events that lead up to this time of which number two is "*the apostasy of the professing church.*" In the New King James notes, they leave that one out. They explain the "*falling away*" as "*the departure.*"

ANSWER #487

In 2 Thessalonians 2:2, the "*day of **Christ**"* is the Received Greek Text Word and is correct, rather than the "*day of the **Lord**"* which is the Gnostic Critical Greek Text word. The Scofield Reference Bible follows the Gnostic Critical Greek Text in many places. In these places, Scofield's editors believed that this Gnostic Critical Greek Text is correct as in this place. In this case, these expressions seem to be synonymous. In any event, "*Christ*" should be used here.

"*Falling away*" would fit the synonymous idea of "*Day of Christ.*" The Greek word APOSTASIA can also mean "*departure.*" Some have interpreted it as such in this place, meaning that this is a reference to the rapture of the born-again Christians to Heaven. This is a controversial subject, of course.

"Taken Up" Or "Cut Loose"?
QUESTION #488

Act 27:40 says: "*And when they had taken up the anchors, they committed themselves unto the sea, and loosed the rudder bands, and hoised up the mainsail to the wind, and made toward shore.*" In the Chinese Union Version (CUV) it changes the clause, "*they had taken up the anchors*" to "*they had cut loose the anchors.*" Does PERIAIREO (4014) have the meaning of "*cut off*"?

ANSWER #488

"*Cut loose*" the anchors would make them useless as anchors. "*Taken up*" or "*taken away*" is more literal, though the results are similar though not the same. HAIREO does not mean "*cut.*" It does mean "*lift up*" or "*take away.*"

4014 periaireo {per-ee-ahee-reh'-o}
from 4012 and 138 (including its alternate); v
AV - take away 3, take up 1; 4
1) **to take away** that which surrounds or envelopes a thing

2) metaph. to take away altogether or entirely
   2a) the guilt of sin, to expiate perfectly

The Meaning Of "Blessed"
QUESTION #489

I'm an ex-Catholic, but now I go to the Gospel Hall here in Toronto. So, coming from Italy, I'm trying to defend the Bible to my brothers, but, they, in turn, tell me that I'm wrong. It's very difficult. Day's ago we were discussing Mary, especially where she says *"henceforth all generations shall call me blessed."* (Luke 1:48). Truly, I don't know how or in what way do I call her blessed, unless I pray to her, but that's not allowed. Another question I have. The people who were blessed in Matthew 5:3 to 11, was the same word used in Greek? If so, does it mean the same thing?

ANSWER #489

In Luke 1:46-49, it is written:

*"And Mary said, My soul doth magnify the Lord, And **my spirit hath rejoiced in God my Saviour**. For he hath regarded the low estate of his handmaiden: for, behold, **from henceforth all generations shall call me blessed**. For he that is mighty hath done to me great things; and holy is his name."*

The same Greek word for *"blessed"* is used in both Luke 1 and Matthew 13. The word is MAKARIOS. Notice that Mary had to have *"God my Saviour."* She needed a *"Saviour"* like every other sinner who ever lived. She is not and never can be a *"co-redemptrix"* as taught by the Roman Catholic Church today.

Here are some of the meanings of the word MAKARIOS translated "blessed" in both Luke and Matthew:

3107 **makarios** {mak-ar'-ee-os}
a prolonged form of the poetical makar (meaning the same);
  TANT - 4:362,548; adj
AV - blessed 44, happy 5, happier 1; 50
1) blessed, happy

This is the meaning. It merely means *"blessed"* or *"happy"* and nothing more. It does not confer a divine nature upon Mary or anyone else mentioned in Matthew 13. For someone to teach that this exalts Mary as the Roman Catholic Church teaches, is to teach heresy.

Meaning Of 1 Thessalonians 1:10
QUESTION #490

I had a couple of questions that I wanted to ask you. In 1 Thessalonians 1:10 the KJB says "*delivered.*" The version of the TR that I have says "RUOMENON." What has happened here? It appears to be a present participle and not a past. Or do I have a wrong version of the TR? Or is my comprehension of the Greek language not good enough?

Also in Luke 2:22 in the TR it says AUTON ("*their*"). But it reads in the KJB AUTES ("*her*"). There is also a note in this TR that says that in the Elzevir text the word is AUTES which would read "*her.*"

ANSWER #490

1 Thessalonians 1:10, you are correct that RUOMENON is a present tense. Dana and Mantey's *Manual Grammar of the Greek New Testament* (pages 181-186) indicates that there are three regular uses of the present tense and five irregular uses. This would be one of the five irregular uses. It is called the "*historical present.*" The King James translators interpreted it as a "*historical present*" which is one of the valid uses of the present tense in Greek grammar.

In Luke 2:22, you do not have a proper TR text. If you have AUTON ("*their*" purification), you have the Gnostic Critical Greek Text reading. This is a textual error. It is also a serious doctrinal heresy. In addition to this, it is contrary to the laws of the Old Testament. Only the mother needed to be purified after the birth of the child, not the father nor the child (Leviticus 12:1-8). If "*their*" purification is used, it implies that the Lord Jesus Christ needed purification. If so, it implies He was a sinner.

Why "Easter" In Acts 12:4?
QUESTION #491

Why do you think that the KJV translates "*passover*" into "*Easter*" that one time? I understand that it is the pagan "*Easter.*"

ANSWER #491

There are a number of possibilities, but the easiest possibility might be to note that Acts 12:3 states these were the "*days of unleavened bread.*" The feast of unleavened bread was celebrated in the first month, the 15th day (Leviticus 23:6). To translate Acts 12:4 as "*after passover*" there is a sequence problem. The feast of passover was celebrated in the first month, the 14th day (Leviticus 23:5). If "*passover*" had already taken place the day before the feast of "*unleavened bread,*" how could it make chronological sense to translate

PASCHA in this case "*passover*"? The Easter pagan feast which took place around the same time as the "*passover*" might have been the reference.

Meaning Of "Disputing"?
QUESTION #492

I came across some questions in regard to Greek words and translating.

Acts 17:17 uses the word "*disputed*." In the footnotes, it mentions "*debated, or argued*"

I then came across Acts 24:12, which Paul claims he was not "*disputing,*" which is what is said was happening in Acts 17:17. So I looked up "*disputed*" and "*disputing*" in my *Word Study* book. It had the same Greek word reference of 1256 in both verses.

Can the word "*disputed or disputing*" have variations of meaning? For instance, in Acts 24:12 it seems Paul was saying that he was not arguing or debating in an angry type of way, whereas in Acts 17:17 it might be taken that way if not also taking into consideration what is said in Acts 24:12, especially with the footnote of Acts 17:17 and its explanation of its meaning "*arguing*." Was it actually in the sense of "*reasoning*," as seems to be explained with Acts 24:12?

ANSWER #492

The meaning of DIALEGOMAI ("*disputed*") in Acts 17:17 is as follows:
1256 **dialegomai** {dee-al-eg'-om-ahee}
middle voice from 1223 and 3004; TANT - 2:93,155; v
AV - dispute 6, reason with 2, reason 2, preach unto 1,
   preach 1, speak 1; 13
1) to think different things with one's self, mingle thought with thought
  1a) to ponder, revolve in mind
2) to converse, discourse with one, **argue**, **discuss**
       DIALOGISMOS ("disputings") as in Philippians 2:14 means as follows:
1261 **dialogismos** {dee-al-og-is-mos'}
from 1260; TANT - 2:96,155; n m
AV - thought 9, reasoning 1, imagination 1, doubtful 1,
   disputing 1, doubting 1; 14
1) the thinking of a man deliberating with himself
  1a) a thought, inward reasoning
  1b) purpose, design
2) a deliberating, questioning about what is true
  2a) hesitation, doubting
  2b) **disputing, arguing**

Meanings Of Five Greek Words
QUESTION #493
What are the proper meanings of these five words below?

1. 1 Corinthians 9:7 *"Who goeth a warfare any time at his own charges?
who planteth a vineyard, and eateth not of the fruit thereof? or who feedeth a
flock, and eateth not of the milk of the **flock**?"*
  Does *"flock"* include *"sheep"* and *"cow"*? That's how it is translated in most
Chinese versions.

2. 2 Corinthians 4:3 *"But if our gospel be hid, it is hid to them that are **lost**."*
  What does the word, *"lost"* mean?

3. 2 Corinthians 5:9 *"Wherefore we **labour**, that, whether present or absent,
we may be accepted of him."*
  Does *"labour"* appear in TR or not?

4. 2 Corinthians 5:11 *"Knowing therefore the terror of the Lord, we
persuade men; but we are made manifest unto God; and I **trust** also are made
manifest in your consciences."*
  "Trust" is translated as *"hope"* in most Chinese versions. We translated it as
"assured reliance."

5. 2 Corinthians 5:14 *"For the love of Christ **constraineth** us; because we
thus judge, that if one died for all, then were all dead:"*
  In most Chinese versions, *"constraineth"* is translated as *"inspire."*

ANSWER #493

1. The word for *"flock"* is POIMNE

4167 **poimne** {poym'-nay}

contraction from 4165; TANT - 6:499,901; n f

AV - flock 4, fold 1; 5

1) a flock (esp.) of sheep

  1a) of Christ's flock i.e. the body of those who follow Jesus as
    their guide and keeper

  The *"flock"* is especially of sheep, but POIMAINO in one place means *"to
feed cattle."*

  This comes from the verb POIMAINO which means:

4165 **poimaino** {poy-mah'-ee-no}

from 4166; TANT - 6:485,901; v

AV - feed 6, rule 4, feed cattle 1; 11

1) to feed, to tend a flock, **keep sheep**

1a) to rule, govern

  1a1) of rulers

  1a2) to furnish pasture for food

  1a3) to nourish

  1a4) to cherish one's body, to serve the body

  1a5) to supply the requisites for the soul's need

For Synonyms see entry 5824

    The clear and usual meaning in the Bible is a "*flock of sheep*." I am not aware that there were "*cattle*" in Jerusalem. When Mrs. Waite and I went there in the 1980's I don't remember seeing any "*cows*" or "*cattle*." We did see some "*goats*."

    2.   Here is the meaning of the Greek word, APOLLUMI, for "*lost*":

622 **apollumi** {ap-ol'-loo-mee}

from 575 and the base of 3639; TANT - 1:394,67; v

AV - perish 33, destroy 26, lose 22, be lost 5, lost 4, misc 2; 92

1) to destroy

  1a) to put out of the way entirely, abolish, put an end to ruin

  1b) render useless

  1c) to kill

  1d) to declare that one must be put to death

  1e) **metaph. to devote or give over to eternal misery in hell**

  1f) to perish, to be lost, ruined, destroyed

2) to destroy

  2a) to lose

    "*Lost*" is a very good translation of APOLLUMI.

    3.   "*Labour*" is in the TR. It is the word, PHILOTIMEOMAI, one of which meanings is of "*labour*."

5389 **philotimeomai** {fil-ot-im-eh'-om-ahee}

middle voice from a compound of 5384 and 5092; v

AV - strive 1, labour 1, study 1; 3

1) to be fond of honour

  1a) to be actuated by love of honour

  1b) from a love of honour **to strive** to bring something to pass

2) to **be ambitious**

  2a) **to strive earnestly**, make it one's aim   DAW

4. The word translated "*trust*" is ELPIZO. It means various things:

1679 <u>elpizo</u> {el-pid'-zo}

from 1680; TANT - 2:517,229; v

AV - trust 18, hope 10, hope for 2, things hoped for 1, hope 1; 32

1) to hope

  1a) in a religious sense, to wait for salvation with joy and
    full confidence

2) hopefully **to trust in**

  "*Trust*" is a valid meaning of ELPIZO as well "*assured reliance*" and other meanings.

---

5. The word for "*constraineth*" is SUNECHO. The meanings are:

4912 <u>sunecho</u> {soon-ekh'-o}

from 4862 and 2192; TANT - 7:877,1117; v

AV - be taken with 3, throng 1, straiten 1, keep in 1, hold 1, stop 1,
    press 1, lie sick of 1, constrain 1, be in a strait 1; 12

1) to hold together

  1a) any whole, lest it fall to pieces or something fall away from it

2) <u>to hold together with constraint</u>, to compress

  2a) to press together with the hand

    2a1) to hold one's ears, to shut the heavens that it may not rain

  2b) to press on every side

    2b1) of a besieged city

    2b2) of a strait, that forces a ship into a narrow channel

    2b3) of a cattle squeeze, that pushing in on each side, forcing
      the beast into a position where it cannot move so the
      farmer can administer medication

3) to hold completely

  3a) to hold fast

    3a1) of a prisoner

  3b) metaph.

    3b1) to be held by, closely occupied with any business

    3b2) in teaching the word

    3b3) <u>to constrain</u>, oppress, of ills laying hold of one and
      distressing him

    3b4) to be held with, afflicted with, suffering from

    3b5) to urge, impel

3b51) of the soul
I don't know how they could make "*inspire*" out of "SUNECHO."
"*Constrain*" is one of the valid meanings of this word.

The Meaning Of "Scarlet"
QUESTION #494

I'm working on a series of lessons on learning KJ contextually and have gotten caught up in a lot of very interesting rabbit trails because of my textile background; one of which is the study of the word, "*scarlet.*" I've attached a file which hopefully will help you answer my questions.

1. Is it correct to say that word #8144 is always plural?

"*8438 Towla represents a worm, a red dye extracted from an insect, Kermes coccus ilicis which deposits its eggs on oak leaves; scarlet is from the cochineal insect of the holm-oak. 8144 shaaniy/shiniy indicates double or repetition;*"

2. On pages 1 and 2 of the attached, I have copied the lexicon numbers for "*scarlet.*" Is it correct to assume the differences in Daniel (7:11) are because of the underlying language being Aramaic rather than the Hebrew?

3. I have for years been troubled about the KJ translation in Proverbs 31:22 as "*silk,*" even without looking at the Hebrew. ("*her clothing is silk and purple.*" This is because of my master's degree is in clothing and textiles and knowing that there is a big difference between silk and linen and the fact that wool and linen were the fibers known to be used by the Hebrews. Egypt was known for its exquisite linens that could be woven so fine that the cloth made from such yarns were transparent; and of course, the Israelites were great sheep herders and thus also used wool. The same number (8336) is used for "*fine linen*" 41 times. This is the same number used in Proverbs 31:22 but translated as "*silk.*"

ANSWER #494

1. Gen. 38:28 looks like a singular, so it is not always "*plural.*"
2. I think this would be a correct conclusion. The Aramaic evidently uses another word.

3. If you look in the *Oxford English Dictionary*, you can see the various meanings of "*silk*" in the 1600's. Like "*brass*" and "*bronze,*" there were various meanings then compared to today.

Various Verse Interpretations

QUESTION #495

1. Is there a kind of parallel between the seven seals in Revelation and the seven feasts of Israel?

2. I was also reading in Hebrews about Melchisedec. His name is in there more. Is that because the folks Paul was writing to were Jewish Christians and it made some kind of point to them?

3. I was wondering why, when folks are writing about Revelation, they seem to compare it to Daniel and not to Genesis?

ANSWER #495

1. I don't think there is anything similar between the seven seal judgments and the seven feasts of the Jews in the Old Testament.

2. Yes, I think the converted Jews, who were the recipients of the book of Hebrews, knew the Old Testament well. So Paul used Melchisedec to illustrate the heavenly Priesthood of our Lord and Saviour Jesus Christ.

3. I think Daniel is quite parallel to Revelation because both books speak of the Last Days. If you're interested in my 44 cassettes, verse by verse sermons on Revelation, you can listen to them. Go to the LINK below on your computer.

http://www.biblefortoday.org/BibleSermons/revelation.htm

"*Which*" or "*Who*"?

QUESTION #496

A pastor preached in Philippians 4:13: "*I can do all things through Christ which strengtheneth me.*" He said it bothered him that some people change the word "*which*" to "*who*." He went on to say that "*which*" was the better choice because, being a demonstrative pronoun it demonstrates Christ rather than pointing to Him. I really don't understand what that meant. He didn't go on to explain.

Since you understand the underlying Greek text, I wondered if you might know where he was trying to go with that thought? Or maybe you understand the reason for the translators using "*which*" rather than "*who*"? I don't remember hearing this addressed before.

ANSWER #496

Regarding "*which*" or "*who*," here is a LINK that might help. http://grammarhound.blogspot.com/2007/08/which-is-it-that-which-or-who. html It gives a short background on it.

In the first place, the way it is used here, it is not a "*demonstrative*" pronoun, but a "*relative pronoun*." According to the *Wikipedia*, "*In English,* *relative pronouns are who, whom, **which**, whose, and that."*

In today's English grammar usage, "*who*" is used with people and "*which*" is used for things. Our present English grammatical rules would make it "Christ Who strengtheneth," because He is a Person. But in 1611, that distinction did not hold. Both "*which*" and "*who*" were used for persons. Here are a few examples:

Genesis 6:4 "*There were giants in the earth in those days; and also after that, when the sons of God came in unto the daughters of men, and they bare children to them, the same became mighty men **which** were of old, men of renown.*"

Genesis 13:5 "*And Lot also, **which** went with Abram, had flocks, and herds, and tents.*"

Genesis 17:21 "*But my covenant will I establish with Isaac, **which** Sarah shall bear unto thee at this set time in the next year.*"

"*Which*" is used 3,881 times in the KJB and usually it refers to "*things*," but (as above and in Philippians 4:13) it also refers to people.

"*Who*" is used only 867 times in the KJB, and seems to be always used with people.

Greek Meaning of "Since"

QUESTION #497

Today, at church, there was a retired minister that spoke while the regular minister was at a family reunion. He gave an excellent message overall, but I did have something that I wanted to ask about that he mentioned. This is in regard to Luke 4:3 and other verses in that chapter where that phrase is mentioned.

The minister said that if going back to the Greek, instead of a question it is actually a statement and mentioned that the Greek word actually says "*since*." "*Since thou art the Son of God*" instead of the KJB translation of "*If thou be the Son of God*" and that it is not actually a question. What is the actual Greek there?

ANSWER #597

The Greek conjunction is EI. According to Greek grammar, it can be properly translated as "*if*" as in the KJB. It can be interpreted either as "*since*" or as "*if.*" Either one is proper and correct. It is not a question, but a part of a compound sentence.

"*Charity*" And "*Love*"

QUESTION #498

I appreciate the research ministry you have. I have one question: Why is the word AGAPE translated as more than one English word i.e. "*charity*" and "*love*?

ANSWER #498

AGAPE is translated sometimes as "*charity*" and sometimes as "*love*." I believe the context was what the King James Bible translators used to determine which term was better in that context. Even today, "*charity*" has a number of meanings: It's still a good word today. Here are some of the definitions of "*charity*."

CHARITY *noun*

1 *Christian Theol.* the love of God for humanity, or a love of one's fellow human beings
2 an act of goodwill or affection
3 the feeling of goodwill; benevolence
4 kindness or leniency in judging others
5 *a*) a voluntary giving of money or other help to those in need *b*) money or help so given *c*) an institution or other recipient of such help
6 a welfare institution, organization, or fund

SYN. MERCY

Etymology

[ME & OFr *charite* derived from L *caritas*, costliness, esteem, affection (in Vulg., often used as transl. of LGr(Ec) *agapÈ*, AGAPE^2) derived from *carus*, dear, valued derived from IE **karo-* derived from base **ka-*, to like, desire]

Use of "Jew" and "Jews"

QUESTION #499

Have you ever heard this theory regarding the word "*Jew*" or "*Jews*" not being translated in the original 1611 AV but only afterward in the 1769 revision & beyond?

ANSWER #499

This is totally false. In the present 1769 KJB, there are 32 uses of "*Jew*" or "*Jews*." I checked the first four references in Esther in the 1611 edition. All four of them have the word, "*Jew*" in them. I am sure that if I took the time to look up the other 28 references, the word, "*Jew*," would be in them as well. I checked also John 4:9. The word, "*Jew*," is there also.

"Waiting" Or "Hoping"?
QUESTION #500

Can you help me understand the Masoretic Hebrew words used in Isaiah 40:30-31 concerning "*waiting upon*" the Lord. Some say it means "*hope in*" and not "*wait upon.*"

ANSWER #500

The Hebrew word can mean "*wait*" all right. No problem. Here are some of the various meanings and translations of the Hebrew word, QAVAH:

06960 **qavah** {kaw-vaw'}

a primitive root; TWOT - 1994,1995; v

AV - wait 29, look 13, wait for 1, look for 1, gathered 1, misc 4; 49

1) **to wait, look for, hope, expect**

  1a) (Qal) waiting (participle)

  1b) (Piel)

    1b1) **to wait or look eagerly for**

    1b2) to lie in wait for

    1b3) to wait for, linger for

2) to collect, bind together

  2a) (Niphal) to be collected

Meaning Of "PORNEIA" (Fornication)
QUESTION #501

What does PORNEIA or "*fornication*" mean in Greek?

ANSWER #501

Here are a few definitions of the Greek noun, PORNEIA, and the verb, PORNEUO. I have also given a LINK to an article below on pornography.

  4202 **porneia** {por-ni'-ah}

from 4203; TANT - 6:579,918; n f

AV - fornication 26; 26

1) illicit sexual intercourse

  1a) adultery, fornication, homosexuality, lesbianism, intercourse
    with animals etc.

  1b) sexual intercourse with close relatives; Lev. 18

  1c) sexual intercourse with a divorced man or woman; Mk. 10:11,12

2) metaph. the worship of idols

  2a) of the defilement of idolatry, as incurred by eating the
    sacrifices offered to idols

    4203 **porneuo** {porn-yoo'-o}

from 4204; TANT - 6:579,918; v

AV - commit fornication 7, commit 1; 8

1) to prostitute one's body to the lust of another
2) to give one's self to unlawful sexual intercourse
   2a) to commit fornication
3) metaph. to be given to idolatry, to worship idols
   3a) to permit one's self to be drawn away by another into idolatry
     http://en.wikipedia.org/wiki/Pornography gives a clear picture of what pornography really is and how it was originally connected with PORNEIA.

Meaning Of HARPAZO & "Rapture"
QUESTION #502

    In a recent newsletter, a man mentions something that I wondered about. He referred to the Latin Vulgate. In reference to 1 Thessalonians 4:13-18, he wrote:

> *"In verse 17, the English phrase 'caught up' translates the Greek word harpazo, which means 'to seize upon with force' or 'to snatch up.' There are those who claim that the word "rapture" isn't in their Bible. That's because they aren't using the Latin translation. The Latin equivalent of the Greek harpazo is the Latin verb 'rapio,' which means 'to take away by force.' In the Latin Vulgate, one of the oldest Bibles in existence, the appropriate tense of 'rapio' appears in verse 17. ('Rapture' is the past participle of 'rapio,' and our English words 'rapt' and 'rapture' stem from this past participle."*

    I just wondered what you thought about the above explanation and the use of the Latin Vulgate?

ANSWER #502

    I believe this is a good summary of the origin of the word, "*rapture.*" This is the meaning of HARPAZO and so it is with the word "*rape*" or the Biblical sense of "*rapture,*" which means "*to take by force.*" This is the meaning of these terms whether in the Latin Vulgate or anywhere else.

    Here are the definitions given by the *Oxford English Dictionary* with many examples in English literature. Notice especially meaning #4 of the 7 meanings given:

rapture, *n.* Also 7 wrap-.
[f. rapt *pa.* pple. + -ure. Cf. *capture.*]
† **1.** The act of seizing and carrying off as prey or plunder. *Obs.*
1608 Shakes. *Per.* ii. I. 161 Spite of all the rapture of the sea, This jewel holds his building on my arm.
c1611 Chapman *Iliad* xxii. 271 Look how an eagle from her height Stoops to the rapture of a lamb.

1639 G. Daniel *Ecclus.* xliv. 6 Who did Realmes subdue...Were wise in Councell, and in Rapture strong.

† **2.** The act of carrying, or fact of being carried, onwards; force of movement. Now *rare*.

1615 Chapman *Odyss.* xiv. 428 Our Ship...'gainst a Rocke, or Flat, her Keele did dash With headlong rapture.

1625 N. Carpenter *Geog. Del.* ii. vi. (1635) 98 A receiued opinion amongst Philosophers..that the sea by the rapture of the heauens should be moued round..in a diurnall course.

1667 Milton *P.L.* vii. 299 Wave rowling after Wave, where way they found, If steep, with torrent rapture.

1888 Lowell *Agassiz* vi. I. 21 With the rapture of great winds to blow About earth's shaken coignes.

† **3. a.** The act of carrying off a woman. *Obs.*

1600 Dekker *Fortunatus* Wks. 1873 I. 151 That feare Which her late violent rapture cast upon her.

1662 J. Bargrave *Pope Alex. VII* (1867) 117 A flat piece of brass, with the rapture of Proserpine by a Centaure.

1728 Newton *Chronol. Amended* I. 114 Under which of the Kings happened the rapture of Europa.

† **b.** = rape *n.*^{2} 3. *Obs.* Also *fig.*

1615 Chapman *Odyss.* xx. 485 My women servants dragg'd about my house To lust and rapture.

1649 G. Daniel *Trinarch., Hen. V,* cccxxix, Though the Representative committ Rapture vpon his heart, in well-drawne Smiles.

4. The act of conveying a person from one place to another, *esp.* to heaven; the fact of being so conveyed.

1647 Ward *Simp. Cobler* 19 Horrid raptures downe to the lowest hell.

1693 J. Edwards *Author. O. & N. Test.* 193 Elias's rapture to heaven.

1842 Manning *Serm.* viii. (1848) 139 In the book of the prophet Ezekiel we read of his rapture to Tel-abib.

1895 A. Nutt *Voy. Bran* I. 273 *note*, The rapture of the hero, by the heroine, to the Underworld.

5. a. Transport of mind, mental exaltation or absorption, ecstasy; now *esp.* ecstatic delight or joy.

1629 Milton *Nativity* 98 Such musick sweet..As all their souls in blisfull rapture took.

1655 Stanley *Hist. Philos.* iii. (1701) 86/1 His Contemplative Rapture at the same time was no less worthy Admiration.

1717 Lady M. W. Montagu *Let. to C'tess Mar* 18 Apr., Women always speak in rapture when they speak of beauty.

1818 M. W. Shelley *Frankenst.* iii. (1865) 58 The astonishment..soon gave place to delight and rapture.

1863 Geo. Eliot *Romola* ii. xxiv, He felt in that moment the rapture and glory of martyrdom without its agony.

b. With *a* and *pl.* An instance of this. (In mod. use the pl. is freq. in the phr. (*to be) in, or (to go) into raptures.*)

1605 Drayton *Bar. Wars* iii. lviii, With such brave raptures from her words that rise, She made a breach in his impressive breast.

1642 Milton *Apol. Smect.* iii. Wks. (1851) 287 This man..sees truth as in a rapture, and cleaves to it.

1738 Wesley *Hymns, 'Again the kind revolving Year'* iv, If aught can there enhance their Bliss Or raise their Raptures higher.

1760 Goldsm. *Cit. W.* xi, He is instantly in raptures at so great an improvement.

1862 M. E. Braddon *Lady Audley* I, A place that strangers fell into raptures with.

1866 Geo. Eliot *F. Holt* (1868) 19 The mother's early raptures had lasted but a short time.

c. A state of passionate excitement; a paroxysm, fit. *rare* (now *dial.*).

1607 Shakes. *Cor.* ii. I. 223 Your pratling Nurse Into a rapture lets her Baby crie.

1634 Sir T. Herbert *Trav.* 24 Then in rage and sudden rapture drew out his knife.

1895 W. C. Fraser *Whaups of Durley* xii, The laddies used to pit her into terrible raptures when they misca'ed her.

d. A strong fit or attack *of* (some emotion or mental state).

1795-1814 Wordsw. *Excurs.* vi. 488 A rapture of forgetfulness.

1871 W. Alexander *Johnny Gibb* ii. 19 'Eh, that's the sea!' exclaimed the lassie in a rapture of admiration.

e. *rapture(s) of the deep or depths,* nitrogen narcosis.

1953 J. Y. Cousteau *Silent World* ii. 14 (*heading*) Rapture of the deep. *Ibid.* 21 We called the seizure *l'ivresse des grandes profondeurs* (rapture, or 'intoxication', of the great depths).

1955 R. & B. Carrier *Dive* iii. 77 This nitrogen narcosis or 'rapture of the depths'..seems to have varying effects on different types of people.

1955 J. Sweeney *Skin Diving & Exploring Underwater* vii. 89 It has not been established with absolute certainty how nitrogen causes a narcotic effect ('raptures of the deep') when breathed under high pressure.

1962 [see *nitrogen narcosis*].

1971 J. F. Bernard tr. *Cousteau's Life & Death in Coral Sea* 261 The diver's threshold of susceptibility to rapture of the depths can be pushed back..by replacing the nitrogen in one's breathing mixture by a lighter gas, such as helium.

1974 *Petroleum Rev.* XXVIII. 672/1 Nitrogen narcosis, popularly called 'raptures of the deep' but perhaps more accurately described as 'the uglies', is the malady caused by nitrogen under pressure, interfering with the normal function of the nervous system.

6. The expression of ecstatic feeling in words or music; a rhapsody.

1620 Melton *Astrolog.* 27 The cause of such Musicall and Harmonious Raptures.

1667 Milton *P.L.* iii. 369 With Præamble sweet..they introduce Thir sacred Song, and waken raptures high.

1763 J. Brown *Poetry & Mus.* vi. 102 When the first Fire of Enthusiasm had vented itself in the Rapture of Hymns and Odes.

1835 Lytton *Rienzi* ix. iv, The people..shouted raptures as he passed.

1845 Browning *Home Th. fr. Abroad* 14 The first fine careless rapture [of the thrush].

7. *Comb.*

a. Instrumental, as *rapture-bound, -bursting, -lightened, -rising, -smitten, -touched, -trembling* adjs.

1842 Faber *Styrian Lake* 26, I see Mary *rapture-bound, And the lily-flowers around.

1824 T. Fenby *Four Temperam.* iv. xv, Its *rapture-bursting joys.

1799 Campbell *Pleas. Hope* Wks. (1837) 6 Turn..thy *rapture-lighten'd eye To Wisdom's walks.

1842 Sir Aubrey de Vere *Song of Faith* 219 With *rapture-rising heart, and a thanksgiving tongue.

1799 Campbell *Pleas. Hope* Wks. (1837) 23 Who hath not own'd with *rapture-smitten frame The power of grace.

1820 T. Mitchell *Aristoph.* I. 209 Your bard shall depart With a *rapture-touch'd heart.

1794 Coleridge *Relig. Musings* vi, Cherubs and *rapture-trembling Seraphim.

b. Objective, as *rapture-breathing, -giving, -moving, -speaking* adjs.

1777 Potter *Æschylus* Suppl. 111 The muses' *rapture-breathing shell.

1787 Burns *Answ. Verses by Guidwife of Wauchope* iv, The saul o' life, the heav'n below, Is *rapture-giving woman.

1801 E. Scot *Alonzo & Cora* 81 Her *rapture-moving voice.

1799 Campbell *Pleas. Hope* Wks. (1837) 4 The *rapture-speaking tear.

Hence

'raptural *a.*, raptu'ration. *nonce-wds.*

1695 Bp. Sprat *Disc. Clergy* 46 Such raptural (if I may so call it) or

Enthusiastical Spirit of Preaching.
a1814 *Gonzanga* ii. I. in *New Brit. Theatre* III. 110 I'll tell you. Now prepare for rapturation.

CHAPTER IV
QUESTIONS ABOUT THE CHINESE ENGLISH VERSION

"Deceit" Or "Error"

QUESTION #503

Here's another question: 1 Thessalonians 2:3 states:
"For our exhortation was not of deceit, nor of uncleanness, nor in guile:"
The Chinese Union Version (CUV) changes *"deceit"* (PLANE) to *"error."*
Which is more accurate?

ANSWER #503

The meanings of PLANE are variously as following::
4106 plane {plan'-ay}
from 4108 (as abstractly); TANT - 6:228,857; n f
AV - error 7, to deceive 1, deceit 1, delusion 1; 10
1) a wandering, a straying about
  1a) one led astray from the right way, roams hither and thither
2) metaph.
  2a) mental straying
    2a1) error, wrong opinion relative to morals or religion
  2b) error which shows itself in action, a wrong mode of acting
  2c) error, **that which leads into error, deceit or fraud**

Notice, one definition is *"that which leads into error, deceit or fraud."* It seems like either *"deceit"* or *"error"* could be used, depending on the context. PLANE is *"error"* all right, but if it is a known *"error"* and is presented to people, it would be rightly called *"deceit."* PLANE is the word from which we get the word *"planet"* which is a wandering heavenly body that moves around, unlike a *"star"* which does not move from place to place.

"Learned Of" Or "Study"?

QUESTION #504

Here's another question about John 6:45 which says:

"It is written in the prophets, And they shall be all taught of God. Every man therefore that hath heard, and hath learned of the Father, cometh unto me."

The phrase, *"Learned of,"* in the Chinese Union Version (CUV) is translated *"study."* Do you think is there another word beside *"study"* to reflect the full meaning of *"learned of"*?

ANSWER #504

As you can see from the meanings below, that the verb, MANTHANO, means *"to learn"* and not *"to study"* You can *"study"* for hours and hours and yet not *"learn"* anything. *"Learning"* is the result of effective *"study,"* but is not identical to it. One is the beginning and the other is the end result.

3129 manthano {man-than'-o}
prolongation from a primary verb, another form of which, matheo,
  is used as an alternate in certain tenses; TANT - 4:390,552; v
AV - learn 24, understand 1; 25
1) to learn, be appraised
    1a) to increase one's knowledge, to be increased in knowledge
    1b) to hear, be informed
    1c) to learn by use and practice
       1c1) to be in the habit of, accustomed to

"Suffereth Violence" In Matt. 11:12

QUESTION #505

I have a question on Matthew 11:12.

"And from the days of John the Baptist until now the kingdom of heaven suffereth violence, and the violent take it by force."

The Chinese Union Version (CUV) translated *"suffereth violence"* as *"struggle"*, or *"try hard"* to enter kingdom of heaven.

"The violent take it by force" is translated *"those try hard will get it."* The word, *"violence,"* is not translated. Can you say this verse in plain English to help us translate it correctly?

ANSWER #505

The meaning of *"suffereth violence"* is
  971 biazo {bee-ad'-zo}
from 979; TANT - 1:609,*; v

AV - suffer violence 1, press 1; 2
1) to use force, to apply force
2) to force, inflict violence on
   The word for "violent" is
973 biastes {bee-as-tace'}
from 971; TANT - 1:613,105; n m
AV - violent 1; 1
1) strong, forceful
2) using force, violent
   The word for "take by force" is
726 harpazo {har-pad'-zo}
from a derivative of 138; TANT - 1:472,80; v
AV - catch up 4, take by force 3, catch away 2, pluck 2,
   catch 1, pull 1; 13
1) to seize, carry off by force
2) to seize on, claim for one's self eagerly
3) to snatch out or away

> I would simply translate it (without interpreting it as follows: "*From or since the days of John the Baptist until now, the kingdom of heaven is forced (on people), and the forceful (or strong) ones seize it away.*" The meaning is not clear, so you must simply translate the words as they are and leave the meaning alone. Sorry that it is so difficult.

"Son" Or "Seed" In Matthew 1:1?
QUESTION #506

Here's another question: Matthew 1:1 "*The book of the generation of Jesus Christ, the son of David, the son of Abraham.*" In the Chinese Union Version (CUV), most of the times the word, "*son*" is translated "*seed*" or "*offspring.*" Do you think there may be some spiritual meaning to use "*son*" instead of "*seed,*" or do you believe that because the Greek uses "*son*" that should be used?

ANSWER #506

The term, "*son*" has many meanings. Here are a few:
1) a son
   1a) rarely used for the young of animals
   1b) generally used of the offspring of men
   1c) in a restricted sense, the male offspring (one born by a father
      and of a mother)
   1d) in a wider sense, a descendant, one of the posterity of any one,
      1d1) the children of Israel

1d2) sons of Abraham
1e) used to describe one who depends on another or is his follower
   1e1) a pupil
2) son of man
   2a) term describing man, carrying the connotation of weakness and mortality
   2b) son of man, symbolically denotes the fifth kingdom in Daniel 7:13 and by this term its humanity is indicated in contrast with the barbarity and ferocity of the four preceding kingdoms (the Babylonian, the Median and the Persian, the Macedonian, and the Roman) typified by the four beasts. In the book of Enoch (2nd Century) it is used of Christ.
   2c) used by Christ himself, doubtless in order that he might intimate his Messiahship and also that he might designate himself as the head of the human race, the man, the one who both furnished the pattern of the perfect man and acted on behalf of all mankind. Christ seems to have preferred this to the other Messianic titles, because by its lowliness it was least suited to foster the expectation of an earthly Messiah in royal splendor.
3) son of God
   3a) used to describe Adam (Lk. 3:38)
   3b) used to describe those who are born again (Lk. 20:36) and of angels and of Jesus Christ
   3c) of those whom God esteems as sons, whom he loves, protects and benefits above others
      3c1) in the OT used of the Jews
      3c2) in the NT of Christians
      3c3) those whose character God, as a loving father, shapes by chastisements (Heb. 12:5-8)
   3d) those who revere God as their father, the pious worshipers of God, those who in character and life resemble God, those who are governed by the Spirit of God, repose the same calm and joyful trust in God which children do in their parents (Rom. 8:14, Gal. 3:26), and hereafter in the blessedness and glory of the life eternal will openly wear this dignity of the sons of God. Term used preeminently of Jesus Christ, as enjoying the supreme love of God, united to him in affectionate intimacy, privy to his saving councils, obedient to the Father's will in all his acts
     If you notice on definition "1d," 1d) in a wider sense, a descendant, one

of the posterity of any one,   1d1) the children of Israel
   1d2) (sons of Abraham)."

> English and Greek both have this sense of "*descendant*" for "*son*." This is the case of "*son of David*" and "*son of Abraham*." If Chinese does not have that meaning of "*son*," you might have to use "*descendant*" or "*seed*."

Questions On Acts 6:6 & 7:30

QUESTION #507

I have questions for following verses:

1) Acts 6:6 says: "*Whom they set before the apostles: and when they had prayed, they laid their hands on them.*"

Could it be translated "*laid their hands on them and prayed*"?

2) Act 7:30 says: "*And when forty years were expired, there appeared to him in the wilderness of mount Sinai an angel of the Lord in a flame of fire in a bush.*"

The Chinese Union Version (CUV) omitted "*of the Lord*." Can KURIOS be translated "*Jehovah*" as in the phrase, "*Jehovah's angel*"?

ANSWER #507

1. Acts 6:6--the order in the Greek is prayed first and laid hands on them second. <u>It would be better to keep the order as the Greek gives it rather than to reverse it</u>.

2. Acts 7:30–<u>The phrase, "*of the Lord*" should be included as in the TR</u>. "*Jehovah*" could be used, but that is Hebrew and O.T. whereas "*Lord*" is proper for KURIOS in the NT. The "*angel of the Lord*" is the phrase used in the OT. I think it is better to use that rather than the "*Lord's angel*" or "*Jehovah's angel*."

"Burdensome" Or "Respect"?

QUESTION #508

Here's another question. I need your help: 1 Thessalonians 2:6 says:
"*Nor of men sought we glory, neither of you, nor yet of others, when we might have been burdensome, as the apostles of Christ.*"

In the Chinese Union Version (CUV), "*burdensome*" is translated as "*respect*." Please advise.

ANSWER 508

The meaning of "*burdensome*" is:
922 barrios {bar'-os}
probably from the same as 939 (through the notion of going down;
  cf 899); TANT - 1:553,95; n n

AV - burden 4, burdensome + 1722 1, weight 1; 6
1) heaviness, weight, burden, trouble
For Synonyms see entry 5819

> We get our English word "*barometer*" from this, which is the measure of "*heaviness*" or "*pressure*."   "*Respect*" is just plain wrong and has no justification as a translation from this Greek word.

Questions On Mark 13:32 & 14:33
QUESTION #509

1)   Mark 13:32 says: "*But of that day and that hour knoweth no man, no, not the angels which are in heaven, neither the Son, but the Father.*"

It has been said that some Greek MSS do not have "*neither the Son,*" and some have these words. What's your opinion? Some have also questioned that God the Son did not know the Father's will wholly during His earthly ministry. What do you believe on this?

2)   Mark 14:33 says: "*And he taketh with him Peter and James and John, and began to be sore amazed, and to be very heavy;*"

The Chinese Union Version (CUV) translated "*sore amazed*" into "*very frightened,*" or "*astounded.*"   What is the Greek's literal meaning of EKTHAMBEO?

ANSWER #509

(1) All Greek MSS editions have "*neither the Son*" or "*nor the Son.*" I believe that the Lord Jesus Christ, as the Son of Man, was not privileged to know "*that hour,*" but the Lord Jesus Christ as the Son of God, was omniscient and knew everything just as God the Father and God the Holy Spirit knew. By His incarnation, the Lord Jesus Christ never gave up any of His Divine attributes, including omniscience.

---

(2) The word, EKTHAMBEO means various things such as:
1568 ekthambeo {ek-tham-beh'-o}
from 1569; TANT - 3:4,*; v
AV - be affrighted 2, sore amazed 1, greatly amazed 1; 4
1) to throw into terror or amazement
  1a) to alarm thoroughly, to terrify
2) to be struck with amazement
  2a) to be thoroughly amazed, astounded
  2b) to be struck with terror

Translation of "ERCHOMAI"
QUESTION #510

The Chinese Union Version (CUV) translated "*should come into.*" John 11:27 says:

"*She saith unto him, Yea, Lord: I believe that thou art the Christ, the Son of God, which **should come into** the world.*"

Can we use the present tense for this?

ANSWER #510

The verb, ERCHOMAI is in the present tense, middle or passive participle in the Greek, so it can be translated as a present tense in both Greek and English. Some of the meanings of ERCHOMAI are listed below.

2064 erchomai {er'-khom-ahee}

middle voice of a primary verb (used only in the present and
  imperfect tenses, the others being supplied by a kindred
  [middle voice] eleuthomai {el-yoo'-thom-ahee}, or [active]
  eltho {el'-tho}, which do not otherwise occur); TANT - 2:666,257; v
AV - come 616, go 13, misc 13, vr come 1; 643
1) to come
 1a) of persons
  1a1) to come from one place to another, and used both of
      persons arriving
  1a2) to appear, make one's appearance, come before the public
2) metaph.
 2a) to come into being, arise, come forth, show itself, find
     place or influence
 2b) be established, become known, to come (fall) into or unto
3) to go, to follow one
For Synonyms see entry 5818

Translating the Chinese Bible
QUESTION #511

1) If the KJB is the only accurate and faithful translation(which I believe), then what about the Chinese Christians? Their Bibles are translated from the Revised version which is corrupt. From my point of view, the Chinese Bible should be translated from the proper Hebrew Words and the proper Greek Words that underlie the King James Bible.

2) Can someone be saved and accepting Christ as their Saviour from a preacher preaching from the corrupt versions other than the KJB?

3) When is the best month to visit New Jersey?

ANSWER #511

(1) The KJB is the only accurate English Bible from the proper Hebrew, Aramaic, and Greek Words. The Chinese Bible needs to be re-translated. This is in progress right now by some Chinese believers. Progress is very slow, however. The Chinese Union Version (CUV) is all the Chinese have, unless they can read an English King James Bible.

(2) <u>Yes, if the gospel is preached and taught plainly with verses that are doctrinally sound rather than the 356 false doctrinal passages.</u>

(3) Probably November (not around Thanksgiving) or December (not around Christmas) would be a good time to visit New Jersey. If you like the shore, you can go in the summer.

Chinese Union Version Like NIV

QUESTION #512

I am compiling a list between CUV (Chinese Union Version), KJV, and NIV. Currently, the Chinese text with English comparison, 99% used NIV. So NIV became the most popular choice. Can you recommend me some good books about the verses comparison and the reasons behind the perversion of God's words.

ANSWER #512

Thanks for your interest in improving the Chinese Bible. I know some have already begun it, but they need all the help they can get to conform it to the Textus Receptus in the New Testament.

I think in the English language, one of the books to see where the Westcott and Hort and the English Revised Version of 1881 departed from the Textus Receptus is my son's book (D. A. Waite, Jr.) called *The Doctored New Testament.* It is BFT #3138 for a gift of $25.00 + $7.00 S&H. You can order by phoning 856-854-4452 with your credit card, or order on line at www.BibleForToday.org if you wish.

This English book is based on the Greek book we have called *Scrivener's Annotated Greek New Testament.* It is **BFT #1670 for a gift of $35.00 + $7.00 S&H.**

Dr. Jack Moorman's book, *8,000 Differences Between the Critical Greek and the Received Greek New Testament* (BFT #3084 @ $20.00 + $7.00 S&H) is the most complete list of differences between the Gnostic Greek text and the Received Greek text. Some of these differences are minor, of course, but there are some very major differences that affect doctrine.

These 8,000 changes involve 356 doctrinal passages where doctrinal errors exist. These places are detailed in a book by Dr. Jack Moorman called *Early Manuscripts, Church Fathers and the Authorized Version* (BFT #3230

$20.00 + $7.00 S&H). There are almost 200 pages listing these 356 doctrinal passages.

I have listed 158 of the more important doctrinal errors of the 356 as found in the NIV, NASV, and other modern versions in Chapter Five of *Defending the King James Bible*. (BFT #1594 for a gift of $12.00 + $7.00 S&H).

Questions On Mark 15:15, 19, & 29

QUESTION #513

1)   Mark 15:15 says: *"And so Pilate, willing to content the people, released Barabbas unto them, and delivered Jesus, when he had scourged him, to be crucified."*

In the Chinese Union Version (CUV,) "HIKANOS" translated to *"to please."* I don't see it is correct. May be more likely *"to satisfy"* or *"to make them content."* Is this right?

2)   Mark 15:19 KALAMOS, is it a *"reed staff"* or a *"cane"*

3)   Mark 15:29: Why is BLASPHEMEO in the KJB translated *"railed"*? Should it be literally translated *"blaspheme"*?

4)   *"third hour"* and *"sixth hour"*

Mark 15:25 *"And it was the third hour, and they crucified him."*

Can I translate to *"And it was nine o'clock, and they crucified him"*?

John 19:14 *"And it was the preparation of the passover, and about the sixth hour: and he saith unto the Jews, Behold your King"*!

And in John 19:14 *"about the sixth hour,"* Can I translate it *"about noon"*?

ANSWER #513

(1)   Though it is difficult because of the two words (poieo hikanos), I believe *"content"* in the KJB meant in 1611 *"to please."*

(2)   I think either is correct: "2563 kalamos {kal'-am-os}; uncertain affinity; n m; AV - reed 11, pen 1; 12; 1) a reed; 2) a staff made of a reed, a reed staff; 3) a measuring reed or rod; 4) a writer's reed, a pen"

(3)   *"railed"* is contained in the verb, BLASPHEMEO, but "blaspheme" is fine. "987 blasphemeo {blas-fay-meh'-o}; from 989; TANT - 1:621,107; v; AV - blaspheme 17, speak evil of 10, rail on 2, blasphemer 1,; speak blasphemy 1, blasphemously 1, misc 3; 35; 1) to speak reproachfully, rail at, revile, calumniate, blaspheme;   2) to be evil spoken of, reviled, railed at"

(4)   It is literally *"third"* and *"sixth"* hour, but since Jews began the day at 6 a.m., 9 o'clock and 12 noon is correct in our time.

"Command" Or "Instruct"?

QUESTION #514

I encountered another difficulty. In the Chinese Union Version (CUV) the following verses all use "*instruct*" where the KJB uses "*command.*"
Matthew 4:3; Luke 9:54

ANSWER #514

You can use "*command*" in all these places rather than "*instruct.*" Instruct is a softer word meaning almost to tell or teach someone something, but command is much more forceful. EIPO is the weakest word for command, but can be used if the context suggests it, as it was suggested eight times in the KJB.

"Might To" Or "In Order To"?

QUESTION #515

In almost all places, I found the clause, "*the prophets might be fulfilled*" translated in the Chinese Union Version (CUV) as "*in order to fulfill.*" Does the Greek have another meaning such as "*so that*" instead of "*in order to*" or "*might be*"?

ANSWER #515

The KJB phrase, "*might be fulfilled*" is from the Greek HINA PLEROTHE. HINA is "*that, or in order that*" and PLEROTHE is the subjunctive mood that is properly translated "*it might be fulfilled.*" The CUV translation of "*in order to fulfill*" would necessitate the "*to fulfill*" to be an infinitive ("*to fulfill*") which is not the case. In general, both translations might be able to pass, but the KJB is more accurate from the literal Greek structure.

"Fornication" & "Adultery" In CUV

QUESTION #516

I found the Chinese Union Version (CUV) sometimes translated differently from the following words in the KJB.

1) Fornication: Mark 7:21 - porneia, Judges 1:7 - ekporneuo?, Revelation 2:14 - porneuo?

2) Adultery: Matthew 19:18 - moicheuo, Hebrews 13:14 - moichos, Matthew 15:19 - moicheia

---

ANSWER #516

Matthew 19:9 describes a Jewish practice of betrothal. During that state, the man was called a "*husband*" and the woman was called a "*wife*." There was no sexual intercourse between them. This betrothal was very binding. It could only be broken by a divorce and the only grounds for such a divorce would be if the other partner had committed fornication. If there was a "*putting away*" or divorce during this betrothal period, (unless one party had committed fornication) followed by a marriage, this would involve "*adultery*." This is why "*fornication*" and "*adultery*" are used in the same verse. They are separate concepts with separate meanings. They are not the same as many Bible teachers and pastors teach.

Omitting "It Came To Pass" In CUV
QUESTION #517

The Chinese Union Version (CUV) dropped most of the uses of "*it came to pass*" as found in the KJB, in Luke. Is this proper?

ANSWER #517

"*It came to pass*" occurs 452 times in our King James Bible. In Hebrew it is WA YAHI. In Greek it is from the verb, GINOMAI. It should be translated every time it occurs to indicate something that either took place, or was about to take place. It is wrong of the CUV to drop out these words.

"Jordan" Or "Jordan River"?
QUESTION #518

In Mark 1:9, the Chinese Union Version (CUV) translated "*Jordan*" as the "*Jordan River*." I found that "*Jordan*" is "*a river of Palestine*." Do you know why the KJB translated to "*in Jordan*"?

Mark 1:9 "*And it came to pass in those days, that Jesus came from Nazareth of Galilee, and was baptized of John **in Jordan**.*"

ANSWER #518

The Greek words are EIS TON IORDANEN which is literally "*in the Jordan*." The "*the*" is often untranslated depending on the sense. But there is no word for "*river*" in the Greek text. That is pure interpretation on the part of the CUV. While it is true that "*Jordan*" is a river, the Bible just literally says "*Jordan*" and not "*Jordan river*.

The Word Order In John 1:12
QUESTION #519

I have some difficulties about John 1:12 which says: *"But as many as received him, to them gave he power to become the sons of God, even to them that believe on his name:"*

The Chinese Union Version (CUV) translates this: *"As those received him, are those who believe on his name, he gave them power to become the children of God."*

I sensed there's some difference between CUV and KJV, but cannot identify correctly. Please help me to compare them. May be the CUV is all right.

ANSWER #519

The CUV changes the order of the Greek clauses for no valid reason. The first clause is all right in order "AS MANY AS RECEIVED HIM." The CUV second clause is out of order. *"believing on His Name"* must come at the end of the verse as the KJB. Other than that, the CUV is somewhat all right, but the KJB is much more literal both in order of the clauses and in accuracy of translation.

Chinese Union Version Verses
QUESTION #520

Here are some questions. Please take time to verify if the Chinese Union Version (CUV) translations are acceptable. It's greatly appreciated.

1) James 4:16: *"But now ye rejoice in your boastings: all such rejoicing is evil."*
The CUV on James 4:16 translates *"rejoicing"* as *"boasting."*

2) 1 John 2:15: *"Love not the world, neither the things that are in the world. If any man love the world, the love of the Father is not in him."*
The CUV on 1 John 2:15 translates *"love"* as Generator or masculine ancestor They translate *"love of the Father"* as *"heart of loving the Father."* We prefer *"Father's love."*

3) 1 John 2:28: *"And now, little children, abide in him; that, when he shall appear, we may have confidence, and not be ashamed before him at his coming."*
The CUV on 1 John 2:28 translates *"confidence"* as *"boldfully fearless."*

ANSWER #520

1) In James 4:16, the Greek word, KAUCHESIS, can mean either *"boasting"* or *"rejoicing"* depending on the context.
kau,chsij **kauchesis** {kow'-khay-sis}

Meaning: 1) the act of glorying
Origin: from 2744; TANT - 3:645,423; n f
Usage: AV - boasting 6, rejoicing 4, glorying 1, whereof I may glory 1; 12

This is the same root word used for "*ye rejoice*" so why not translate it "*rejoice*" in the last part of the verse.

2) In 1 John 2:15. Your translation is accurate Greek, theirs is erroneous. There is no word for "*heart*" in the Greek. They are using dynamic equivalence here.

3) In John 2:28 Here is the word for "*confidence*." It is PARRHESIA. parrhsi, a parrhesia {par-rhay-see'-ah}
Meaning: 1) freedom in speaking, unreservedness in speech 1a) openly, frankly, i.e without concealment 1b) without ambiguity or circumlocution 1c) without the use of figures and comparisons 2) free and fearless **confidence**, cheerful courage, boldness, assurance 3) the deportment by which one becomes conspicuous or secures publicity
Origin: from 3956 and a derivative of 4483; TANT - 5:871,794; n f
Usage: AV - boldness 8, **confidence** 6, openly 4, plainly 4, openly + 1722 2, boldly + 1722 1, misc 6; 31

"*Confidence*" is within the meanings of PARRHESIA very definitely. The CUV is not good.

1 John 2:15--Chinese Union Version
QUESTION #521
1 John 2:15, can we translate "*love of the Father*" as "*love from the Father*"? This is quite different from the Chinese Union Version (CUV) translation of "*the heart of loving the Father.*" What do you think?

ANSWER #521
1 John 2:15 states: "*Love not the world, neither the things that are in the world. If any man love the world, the love of the Father is not in him.*"

In the phrase, "*the love of the Father is not in him,*" the word, "*Father,*" is in the genitive case in Greek. There are two senses of the genitive. (1) one is subjective genitive ("*The Father's love*") and (2) the other is the objective genitive ("*The love for the Father.*").

Either are correct. I believe the context dictates "*love for the Father.*" "*The heart of loving the Father*" has no place in the translation. Though it takes the objective genitive position as I do, there is no support whatsoever from the Greek for "*the heart.*" This is pure addition to the Words of God and should be rejected.

Chinese Union Version Problems
QUESTION #522

Here're three questions; please help us to resolve:

1) KJB Revelation 16:3 *"And the second angel poured out his vial upon the sea; and it became as the blood of a dead man: and **every** living soul died in the sea."*

CUV   (The Chinese Union Version) 16:3

*"...**every living soul** died in the sea."* CUV translated to *"...living things **all** died in the sea."* We intend to translate to *"...**every living soul**..."* as the KJV. We believe KJV is correct?

2) Revelation 18:13 *"And cinnamon, and odours, and ointments, and frankincense, and wine, and oil, and fine flour, and wheat, and beasts, and sheep, and horses, and chariots, and slaves, and **souls of men.**"*

CUV   18:13

*"**souls of men**"* CUV translated to *"**people**"*, we intend to translate to *"**souls**"* as KJV.

3) I am not sure if I asked you before about this question.

Revelation 20:4   *"And I saw thrones, and they sat upon them, and judgment was given unto them: and I saw the souls of them that were beheaded for the witness of Jesus, and for the word of God, and which had not worshipped the beast, neither his image, neither had received his mark upon their foreheads, or in their hands; and they lived and **reigned with Christ** a thousand years."*

CUB   20:4

CUV translated *"**reigned** with Christ"* as *"**to be king** with Christ."* Is this correct?

ANSWER #522

As for your three questions, let me say this:

1. Since the *"all"* (PASA) comes first in the clause, I would keep the same order of the words that the KJB has followed.

2. The word, PSUCHE, translated *"souls"* in both these verses has many meanings such as:

5590 psuche {psoo-khay'}

from 5594; TDNT - 9:608,1342; n f

AV - soul 58, life 40, mind 3, heart 1, heartily + 1537 1, not tr 2; 105

1) breath

 1a) the breath of life

  1a1) the vital force which animates the body and shows itself
   in breathing

```
      1a1a) of animals
      1a12) of men
  1b) life
  1c) that in which there is life
      1c1) a living being, a living soul
```

2) **the soul**

  2a) the seat of the feelings, desires, affections, aversions
      (our heart, soul etc.)

  2b) the (human) soul in so far as it is constituted that by
      the right use of the aids offered it by God it can attain
      its highest end and secure eternal blessedness, the soul
      regarded as a moral being designed for everlasting life

  2c) the soul as an essence which differs from the body and is not
      dissolved by death (distinguished from other parts of the body)

"**souls of men**" is exactly what the Greek has literally. (PSUCHAS ANTHROPON), so you're right on target here.

   3. The word "*reigned*" (BASILEUO) has various meanings such as the following:

936 basileuo {bas-il-yoo'-o}
from 935; TDNT - 1:590,97; v
AV - **reign** 20, king 1, 21
1) to be king, to exercise kingly power, to reign
  1a) of the governor of a province
  1b) of the rule of the Messiah
  1c) of **the reign** of Christians in the millennium
2) metaph. to exercise the highest influence, to control

Though "*to be king*" is possible, this would mean that every Christian would be a king. This is false in this context. Only the Lord Jesus Christ is the King of Kings and Lord of Lords. Christians will "*reign with Him*," but we will not usurp His Kingship. You and the KJB are correct in this.

Chinese Union Version Questions

QUESTION #523

Here're two questions:

1) Revelation 21:24 "*And the **nations** of them which are saved shall walk in the light of it: and the kings of the earth do bring their glory and honour into it.*"
CUV 21:24

CUV translated *"nations"* to *"all nations."* Can we translate it as *"people"* instead?

2) Revelation 22:16 *"I Jesus have sent mine **angel** to testify unto you these things in the churches. I am the root and the offspring of David, and the bright and morning star."*

CUV 22:16

CUV translated *"angel"* as *"messenger."* Can we translate it as *"angel"*?

ANSWER #523

Let me give some comments on your two questions:

1. Revelation 21:24 Here are some of the meanings involved:

1484 **ethnos** {eth'-nos}

probably from 1486; TDNT - 2:364,201; n n

AV - Gentiles 93, nation 64, heathen 5, people 2; 164

1) a multitude (whether of men or of beasts) associated or
   living together
   1a) a company, troop, swarm
2) a multitude of individuals of the same nature or genus
   2a) the human race
3) a race, **nation**, **people group**
4) in the OT, foreign nations not worshipping the true God, pagans,
   Gentiles

5) Paul uses the term for Gentile Christians

You could use *"people"* for ETHNOS though it is usually used for Gentile people as opposed to Jews. The thing that the Chinese Union Version (CUV) leaves out, perhaps, is the phrase *"**of them which are saved**."* If so, (and it probably is) it is serious "universalism." These words are omitted from the Gnostic Critical Text and the ERV, NASV, NIV, NASV, RSV, NRSV, ESV, and almost all of the modern English versions.

2. Revelation 22:16

32 **aggelos** {ang'-el-os}

from aggello [probably derived from 71, cf 34] (to bring tidings);
   TDNT - 1:74,12; n m

AV - angel 179, messenger 7; 186

1) a messenger, envoy, one who is sent, **an angel**, a **messenger from God**

Certainly the transliterated *"angel"* is acceptable to use. It is known by all people that it is a *"divine messenger,"* not just some human *"delivery boy."*

Chinese Union Version Questions
QUESTION #524

Please advise us about the following three verses:

1) Matthew 6: 22 "*The light of the body is the eye: if therefore thine eye be **single**, thy whole body shall be full of light.*"
The Chinese Union Version (CUV) translated "**single**" to "**bright**." We are divided on two opinions: a) "*healthy*," b) "*pure*." What are your choices?

2) Matthew 6:23 "*But if thine eye be **evil**, thy whole body shall be full of darkness. If therefore the light that is in thee be darkness, how great is that darkness!*"
The Chinese Union Version (CUV) translated "**evil**" to "**dim-sighted**." We prefer "**evil**" literally. What do you think?

3) Matthew 5:28 "*But I say unto you, That whosoever looketh on a woman to **lust** after her hath committed adultery with her already in his heart.*"
The Chinese Union Version (CUV) translated "*looked on a woman*" then "*to lust*." We prefer "*to lust*" as the "*cause*." Is this right?

ANSWER #524

1. In Matthew 6:22, here is the word translated as "**single**":
573 **haplous** {hap-looce'}
probably from 1 (as a particle of union) and the base of 4120;
 TDNT - 1:386,65; adj
AV - single 2; 2
1) simple, **single**
2) **whole**
3) good **fulfilling its office, sound**
   3a) of the eye
   I would use "*whole*" or "*sound*" or "*fulfilling its office*."
2. Matthew 6:23:

The various meanings of PONEROS are:
4190 **poneros** {pon-ay-ros'}
from a derivative of 4192; TDNT - 6:546,912; adj
AV - **evil** 51, wicked 10, wicked one 6, evil things 2, misc 7; 76
1) full of labours, annoyances, hardships
  1a) pressed and harassed by labours
  1b) bringing toils, annoyances, perils; of a time full of
     peril to Christian faith and steadfastness; causing pain and
     trouble

2) bad, of a bad nature or condition

  2a) in a physical sense: diseased or blind

  2b) in an ethical sense: <u>evil</u> wicked, bad

The word is used in the nominative case in Mt. 6:13. This usually denotes a title in the Greek. <u>Hence Christ is saying, deliver us from "*The Evil*", and is probably referring to Satan.</u>

I think you should stick to some form of "*evil*," "*wicked*," or "*bad*." I agree with you on this.

3. Matthew 5:28

The structure of PROS + EPITHUMEO seems to imply "*looking*" (BLEPO) "*in order to or for the purpose of lusting*" Yes, the "*cause*" of adultery in the heart is "looking on a woman for the purpose of lusting after her."

CHAPTER V
QUESTIONS ABOUT
VARIOUS BIBLE VERSIONS

Geneva Bible & Jay Green
QUESTION #525

1. What do you think of the Geneva Bible?

2. What is unreliable about the Jay Green Interlinear? Since I now own a copy,(my sister gave it to me), I would appreciate you letting me know what to be wary of.

ANSWER #525

1. I have not reviewed the Geneva Bible. The KJB translator, John Reynolds asked the King of England for another translation, "*The ones extant* (in existence then) *not answering to the originals*." This included the Geneva version, which was then extant, so, in the opinion of John Reynolds, it "*did not answer to the originals*" as closely as it should.

2. The only purpose for Green's *Interlinear*, or any other interlinear Bible, is to see what Greek and Hebrew Words underlie the KJB so people can look them up in a Lexicon. Though Jay Green's *Interlinear* includes a good Greek text (Beza's 5th edition, 1598 used by Scrivener), it has Green's own defective translation in the margins rather than the King James Bible.

Bible Versions Controversy Basics
QUESTION #526

Could you please suggest which of yours or your colleagues' book(s) would best present the basics of the KJV vs. the other Bible versions controversy?

ANSWER #526

I would suggest you begin with my own book, *Defending the King James Bible* which is **BFT #1554** and can be ordered online at **$12.00 plus $7.00 S&H**. The Appendix has over 1,000 other titles defending the King James

Bible and its underlying Hebrew, Aramaic, and Greek Words. I could give you other helpful titles as well. You can reach the BFT Web page to order this book if you wish at BibleForToday.org.

You can find the DBS Speakers' Index that you wanted on this link: http://www.biblefortoday.org/idx_dbs_video_sermons.htm.

American Standard Version Critique
QUESTION #527

I have been searching for some time for a complete list of changes to the Old Testament of the American Standard Version (ASV). Do you have such a list? I appreciate any and all help you can give. Many thanks and keep up the defense work for the KJV.

ANSWER #527

The only things I have on the ASV are as follows

BFT #1857 240pp. $12.00   Inside Story Of The Anglo American A.S.V. & R.S.V. Coy, George H.

BFT #0986 84pp. $8.50   ASV, NASV & NIV Departures from Traditional Hebrew/Greek Texts

I do not have a complete list as I have for the NKJV, NASV, and NIV.

Bible Translation Reviews
QUESTION #528

Where is your best source of Bible translation reviews? Do you comment on modern English-language versions of the entire Bible, Old and New Testaments, or partial versions, such as versions of the OT, Psalter, or just the NT in English?

If you have written any books in which you give your view of the KJV and other Bibles such as RSV, NSRV, NKJV, ESV, NASB, NIV, TEV, ASV, CEV, NLT, AMP, HCSB, NEB, REB, and so on, please let me know, if you would.

ANSWER #528

I have written some extensive reviews on the KJB original vs. the present KJB, on the NKJV, on the NASV, and on the NIV. I don't know anyone who is reviewing versions extensively.

I oppose any and all of the Bible versions (which involves over 99.5% of them, and including all of the ones you mentioned). I oppose them because they are based on the Gnostic Critical Texts of either Westcott and Hort, Nestle-Aland, or United Bible Societies. These Greek Texts make over 8,000 changes in the Greek Words underlying the King James Bible New Testament.

Though some of these changes are minor and some do not make any change in English, there are 356 passages which are doctrinal and therefore important changes. This is in addition to their inferior translators, their inferior dynamic equivalency translation technique, and their inferior theology.

After my extensive Genesis through Revelation reviews above, I think it is a waste of my time to continue this effort with other versions.

I have done brief analyses of the *Today's New International Version* (NIVILE), *Holes in the Holman Bible* (HCSB), the Contemporary English Version (CEV), and the American Standard Version (ASV).

I don't know of others (though I am sure there are a few) who critique these versions based on the above standards.

Jay Green's *Interlinear Bible*
QUESTION #529

I recently received the *Interlinear Bible* (Greek, Hebrew, English), by Jay P. Green Sr., published 1978 by Hendrickson. As I began looking into it, I noticed what looks to be errors in the AV, they are in Matt. 2:4, where Herod asks, in the Greek linear, "*Where should 'the Christ' be born?*" In the King James Version he asks "*Where should Christ be born?*". And another is in Genesis 3:5 the KJV renders "*as gods*" rather than "*like God,*" as in the interlinear? The introduction to this interlinear claims the use of the Received and Masoretic manuscripts, and even debunks the new versions. So I felt safe in using it, knowing the source.

My question is, why did the KJ translators change these two verses? I suppose there to be a good reasoning behind it, and as I am a defender of the AV, and have read it with the assurance that it is a God-blessed translation, I feel I must have an answer for this. I do hope you can help me understand this, as I have talked with defenders of other versions, one of their claims is to accuse the KJ translators of altering the text, knowing doctrinally they have not, yet this is a little stumbling block in the road for me.

ANSWER #529

I would not rely on the translations under the Hebrew or Greek words in Jay Green's *Interlinear*. The KJB is correct. It is Jay Green's error and change from the KJB. Though the Greek is "HO CHRISTOS" which is literally "*the Christ,*" yet the translation of the article "*the*" is not always needed in English as in the KJB

In Genesis 3:5, the Hebrew word is ELOHIM which, depending on whether it refers to the true God or heathen gods, can be taken for either, depending on the context. Since the serpent (Satan) does not recognize the true

God, perhaps the KJB men made it heathen "*gods.*" The same is true in Daniel 3:25 where our Bible uses for ELOHIM "*the son of God*" but many wrongly use "*a son of the gods*" for the same words.

I wouldn't be concerned about either of these instances since they are all within the parameters of good choices from the Greek and Hebrew Words from which they are taken. Context and interpretation are involved in all of them.

A Sound Italian Bible?

QUESTION #530

I am searching for an Italian Bible for study and ministry, but I am unsure of the most accurate translation to use. I have purchased a number of *Defined King James Bibles* from BFT and currently use these for my primary Bible study and reading. I have an additional need to find the best available translation in Italian. Could you recommend for me an Italian Bible translation and a source for obtaining copies?

ANSWER #530

I do not know of a good Italian N.T. or Bible. I know that the Giovani Diodati version of 1607 was a good one in its day, but I don't know if it is still in print. You might check if this is still available. For $14.95, you can order this at http://www.logos.com/ebooks/details/IT-DIODATI1649 if you wish.

The Webster Bible Vs. KJB

QUESTION #531

I have a quick question about the KJB. I have come across a text that is dated in 1850. To my knowledge we have always traditionally used and printed the 1769 King James Bible text. Attached is a document that shows the differences between the 1850 and the 1769. I'm just curious more than anything else about your thoughts on it. As for the 1850 text, I have never seen anything like it, and was unable to find anything that even spoke of an 1850 edition of the King James Bible. Perhaps someone down the line has missed the date or something. I got this text out of the original E-Sword Bible program which can be found here: www.e-Sword.net and they are the ones that give the date 1850. Any thoughts or information on this would be appreciated. I started highlighting some of the differences between the two, but have not done an exhaustive comparison of the two. Thank you for taking the time to look at this.

ANSWER #531

I compared the readings of a few that you gave with *The Webster Bible* by Noah Webster, dated 1833. I believe by and large this 1850 KJB is just updating the spelling of the words which were uncommon in their day much like the NKJV sought to do (plus many additional word changes). In almost all examples I looked at, the *Webster Bible* updated the spelling as the 1850. "bare" vs. "bore," "a" vs. "an," "begot" vs. "begat," etc.

I wouldn't trust the update because in almost 800,000 words found in the King James Bible, they might have made a mistake or two, or even several thousands. The changes are slight and only spellings that I noted. For anything of a serious nature, the *Defined King James Bible* is all we need.

Why Differences In Bible Versions?

QUESTION #532

My information is that the original manuscripts, Hebrew, Aramaic, and Greek are no longer in existence. This means that all *"versions"* of the Bible we use today were translated from copies of the original manuscripts.

That being so, are all Bible versions translated from the same language and dialect? If so, why do I see opposite messages in Scripture from different Bible versions?

Example: Exodus 21:2 *"If thou buy an Hebrew **servant**, six years he shall serve: and in the seventh he shall go out free for nothing."* (KJV)

Exodus 21:2 *"When you buy a Hebrew **slave**, he shall serve six years, and in the seventh he shall go out free, for nothing."* (RSV)

I am not a student of Hebrew. The Hebrew word "EBED" does not show *"slave"* as one of its definitions. So, how did *"slave"* get into Exodus 21:2 in the RSV?

ANSWER #532

In answer to your question, *"are all Bible versions translated from the same language and dialect?"* The answer is "No." Except for the King James Bible, most of the versions in English and in other languages (with a very few exceptions) are taken from inferior Hebrew and Aramaic copies for the Old Testament and inferior Gnostic Critical Greek Text copies for the New Testament. In fact, the Gnostic Critical Greek New Testament words have over 8,000 differences from those Traditional Text Words underlying the King James Bible. Of these 8,000 differences, though some are minor, there are over 356 doctrinal passages that are included. These passages are very important.

As for the word EBED, here are the various meanings of it as found in Exodus 21:2:
05650 `ebed {eh'-bed}

from 05647; TWOT - 1553a; n m

AV - servant 744, manservant 23, bondman 21, bondage 10, bondservant 1,
  on all sides 1; 800

1) slave, servant

  1a) slave, servant, man-servant

  1b) subjects

  1c) servants, worshipers (of God)

  1d) servant (in special sense as prophets, Levites etc)

  1e) servant (of Israel)

  1f) servant (as form of address between equals)

Young's Literal Translation

QUESTION #533

What do you think of Robert *Young's Literal Translation* of the Bible that came out in 1898? It claims to come from the same original Greek Received Text as the King James, I'm not sure about the Old Testament. It reads easily. Mine is said to be a revised version by the publishers which sounds like bad news to me. Young writes, in the preface, (1) That he has restored the verb tenses of the original manuscripts; (2) That he uses modern English words for each differing Greek or Hebrew word rather than selecting one word to represent many similar words as he says the King James does; (3) He does not claim to replace the King James but sites his as a companion volume though he calls the King James translators "*revisers*." What do you think of it?

ANSWER #533

I have a copy of Young's literal translation, but do not use it or consult it. Yes, it is supposed to come, in the New Testament, from the Traditional Text. But I would not trust it against the King James Bible. It was probably the "*new*" King James Version of his day. Our answer to "*modern English words*" is our *Defined King James Bible* which doesn't change a single KJB word, but only adds explanatory footnotes for uncommon words. This keeps a unity of Bible version for use in a church congregation rather than having, as in many churches today, many conflicting versions.

LUCIFER, BJU, & The ESV

QUESTION #534

I wrote a letter to Stephen Jones, President of Bob Jones University. He said Lucifer never appeared before the Vulgate translation. He also said that "*Day Star*" is an accurate Hebrew translation for "*Lucifer*" in Isaiah 14:12. He claimed that no royalties are now being paid to the NCC for every copy of the ESV that's sold.

ANSWER #534

It is interesting that Steven Jones admitted the ESV publishers had to pay $625,000 to the apostate group that holds the copyright on the error-ridden RSV text in order to modify it.

Neither "*day star*" nor "*morning star*" are accurate translations of the Hebrew word, HEYLEL in Isaiah 14:12. It means a "*shining one*" or "*light-bearer.*" There is no Hebrew word in this verse either for "*day,*" or "*star*" or "*morning.*" On the other hand, "*Lucifer*" is an excellent translation for HEYLEL. "*Lucifer*" is a compound Latin word made up of LUX ("*light*") and FERO ("*to bear or carry*"). "*Lucifer*" literally means "*light bearer.*" That is exactly what the Hebrew word, HEYLEL, means.

What's Wrong With The NKJV?

QUESTION #535

Please give me information about your knowledge about the NKJV. It is one modern translation which was taken from the Textus Receptus. Why is it not accurate in its translation?

Is there any recent translation that is totally true and faithful to the same text as the KJV which uses more contemporary English?

One area I find to be a dilemma is the ability to translate second person pronouns such as translated "*ye*" in the KJV. How could that possibly be translated in modern English since we normally use "you" as both singular and plural. Since I am from Texas, it could be translated "y'all", but it might not catch on very well where you live.

ANSWER #535

My book analyzing the *New King James Version* (**BFT #1442** ($10.00 + $7.00 S&H)) goes into the over 2,000 places where the NKJV is defective. It is mostly TR, but I found three places, by accident, that it is the Gnostic Critical Greek Text. Another man found over 100 more places. In any event, the NKJV is not faithful to the Hebrew, Aramaic, or Greek Words that underlie it in at least these over 2,000 places.

There is no faithful contemporary version in the English language that is faithful to the Traditional Hebrew, Aramaic, and Greek Words underlying the King James Bible. This includes the New King James Version which has over 2,000 examples of dynamic equivalence paraphrases.

Thee, thy, thine, on the one hand, and ye, you (as object), and other distinctive words are needed to determine easily singulars and plurals. An example of why this is needed is found in John 3:7: "*Marvel not that I said unto thee, Ye must be born again.*" The Lord Jesus Christ was talking to one man,

Nicodemus. That is the "*thee*" singular. The "*ye*" refers to all the Pharisees in the party of Nicodemus. Other versions use "*you*" for both these singular and plural instances, thus blurring the important distinctions. If virtually all the languages in the world have separate pronouns for singular "*you*" and plural "*you*," why not English?

Good Study Bibles
QUESTION #536

Do you carry any good study Bibles with biblically correct commentary? I have found that it is difficult to find trustworthy study bibles.

ANSWER #536

We don't carry "*study Bibles*" in the usual sense, though our *Defined King James Bible* studies uncommon words which no other Bible does in such a complete manner. In that way, it is a "*study Bible*" of a different sort from commentary.

Failures Of The NIV
QUESTION #537

We really need to pray for this. Last night during our Bible study, I and another member suggested on the next meeting that we study the different versions of the Bible. And, she mentioned NIV and I agreed. We were attacked and mocked, especially me. Because they knew I was an adamant King James Bible defender. I have to confess that I lost my temper and blurted out during the attack that "*why would I advocate using the NIV if I knew it is a corrupt version and anyone doing so knowing that it is wrong will be judged.*

I did a lot of research on the NIV sometime 3-5 years ago. I have a bagful of papers but I could not find the pages of the names of the NIV Translators. I know one of them is Virginia Mollenkott who was a Lesbian. Do you have their names and their backgrounds? If it is available would you send it to me? Just let me know how much it will cost.

ANSWER #537

We have the list of translators and helpers who made up the New International Version (NIV). We can send it to anyone who asks us for it.

I have enclosed an article about the NIV which is helpful in understanding some of its defects. The title is: "*Which Bible Verses did the NIV Delete*?" Anonymous, located October 6, 2006

Several readers have asked me this question so I thought it worthwhile to include my response here. Please note that these are only WHOLE verses that the NIV deletes. This list does not include the many words and phrases that were completely deleted from the NIV--it deletes over 64,000 words including words like mercyseat, Jehovah, and Godhead. It removes meaningful, well-known Bible words like Calvary, Lucifer, new testament, regeneration, etc. Most of the modern Bibles line up very closely with the NIV--and so does the New World Translation--the Bible of the Jehovah's Witnesses which predates the NIV!

> When you read below where I say that a verse is COMPLETELY deleted, I mean clean/bald-headed/gone/vanished deleted. For instance, if you search for Acts 8:37 in the NIV you will read,
>
> 36 *As they traveled along the road, they came to some water and the eunuch said, "Look, here is water. Why shouldn't I be baptized?"*
>
> 38 *And he ordered the chariot to stop. Then both Philip and the eunuch went down into the water and Philip baptized him.*
>
> Verse 37 is gone and vanished. It is a powerful verse! Some foolish people have written me saying, "But it says something in the footnotes." I have three responses.

(1) When you are reading your Bible do you look at the footnotes after every verse? Do you say "I am reading verse 3 so let me look below and see if something in verse 3 is missing."? Even if you did do that (which you don't) the footnotes say that the "*best manuscripts*" don't have the verse--will you then agree with them that the verse doesn't belong? If not, then why are you reading an NIV?

(2) Not all the word deletions are found in the footnotes of the NIV so don't think for a second that they are letting you know all the changes they made.

(3) The next logical step will be for the NIV to omit the footnotes and just reorder everything. In the example above, verse 38 would become verse 37 so it wouldn't look funny. Look at the J.B. Phillips translation--that heretick didn't number the individual verses so you don't know what you're missing. It's paragraph style. The NIV may go that way too. They are desensitizing you to the changing of the very words of God. In summary, they'll either renumber or go to that paragraph format.

Wait a minute, hold the presses! I got the following from one of our readers:

"*I was in the Christian Book store today. I saw some thing that shocked me. I look through the Bibles often. I looked at the CHILDREN'S NIV. I looked up the missing verses and there was something I could not believe. I looked up Matt 17:21 and of course it is missing BUT in this Children's Bible it was typed out like this 20/21 and the 21st verse was still missing. They make you think that you read the 21st verse but it still is just the 20th verse! Can you believe it???!!! If you want to look for yourself find the CHILDREN'S NIV BIBLE, and see for yourself. I did look in the other NIV's to see if they did the same thing. They DID NOT do that, BUT how long before they do?????!"*

They are already sneaking the deletions into the children's Bibles! This is the second time that I've heard of those foxes pulling one over on little helpless children. The other thing I've seen them do is retranslate the kids' and prisoners' Bibles to make them gender neutral. Of course those foxes didn't market them that way, they just snuck in the gender inclusivity. See this article for details.

Another update! I just opened the JW "Bible," the New World Translation (1961 ed.), and looked up all the verses that the NIV completely deletes. The Jehovah's Witness Bible deletes the exact same ones!!!! I mean all of them! The only difference between the NIV and the New World Translation deletions is that the JW Bible does not include any footnotes! Isn't that what I said above, that the NIV would eventually delete the footnotes? To learn more about the Jehovah's Witnesses and their damnable doctrines go to our article on cults.

Our illiterate, lazy culture has spilled over to many professing Christians who have embraced the ways of the sluggard (and their want shall come upon them as an armed man). They are willing to read a Satanic "Bible" version missing what God says so they can be lazy and not do their due diligence. Your modern Bible perversion was written by men using dynamic equivalence. In other words, they are telling you their interpretation and their doctrine--NOT what the manuscripts really say. Don't believe me? Look at the article on the NIV using gender inclusive language. Gender inclusivity wasn't in the "originals"--it is a modern, feminist concept born of rebellion.

A number of brothers and sisters, after examining the facts, have said, "*I'm getting a King James!*" Many have shared what a blessing the King James Bible has been to them and their spiritual life. The King James isn't hard. I've seen one and two year olds quoting it and I am not exaggerating. I've taught it to people who cannot read and to children whose second language is English. I actually find the modern Bibles more difficult to read than the King James.

If you read a modern Bible, don't let your pride get in the way of really looking at this information. Some people get hostile because I'm sharing these facts. Look up the verses and see that what you call the Bible is not the Bible. Get a real Bible. The King James conformable to the edition of 1611--NOT the New King James or the KJ21, etc. they are not King James Bibles.

WHOLE Bible verses deleted in the NIV

The following WHOLE verses have been removed in the NIV--whether in the text or footnotes...over 40 IN ALL!!!

Here are 23 references of these 40 for you to see:

1. Matthew 12:47--removed in the footnotes

2. Matthew 17:21--**COMPLETELY** removed [also deleted from the Jehovah's Witness "Bible"]. What are you NIV readers missing? *"Howbeit this kind goeth not out but by prayer and fasting."*

3. Matthew 18:11--**COMPLETELY** removed [also deleted from the Jehovah's Witness "Bible"]. What are you NIV readers missing? *"For the Son of man is come to save that which was lost."*

4. Matthew 21:44--removed in the footnotes

5. Matthew 23:14--**COMPLETELY** removed [also deleted from the Jehovah's Witness "Bible"]. What are you NIV readers missing? *"Woe unto you, scribes and Pharisees, hypocrites! for ye devour widows' houses, and for a pretence make long prayer: therefore ye shall receive the greater damnation."*

6. Mark 7:16--**COMPLETELY** removed [also deleted from the Jehovah's Witness "Bible"]. What are you NIV readers missing? *"If any man have ears to hear, let him hear."*

7. Mark 9:44--**COMPLETELY** removed [also deleted from the Jehovah's Witness "Bible"]. What are you NIV readers missing? *"Where their worm dieth not, and the fire is not quenched."*

8. Mark 9:46--**COMPLETELY** removed [also deleted from the Jehovah's Witness "Bible"]. What are you NIV readers missing? *"Where their worm dieth not, and the fire is not quenched."*

9. Mark 11:26--**COMPLETELY** removed [also deleted from the Jehovah's Witness "Bible"]. What are you NIV readers missing? *"But if ye do not forgive, neither will your Father which is in heaven forgive your trespasses."*

10. Mark 15:28--**COMPLETELY** removed [also deleted from the Jehovah's Witness "Bible"]. What are you NIV readers missing? *"And the scripture was fulfilled, which saith, And he was numbered with the transgressors."*

11. Mark 16:9-20 (all 12 verses) -- There is a line separating the last 12 verses of Mark from the main text. Right under the line it says: [*"The two most reliable early manuscripts do not have Mark 16:9-20"*] (NIV, 1978 ed.) The Jehovah's Witness "Bible" also places the last 12 verses of Mark as an appendix of sorts.

12. Luke 17:36--**COMPLETELY** removed [also deleted from the Jehovah's Witness "Bible"]. What are you NIV readers missing? *"Two men*

shall be in the field; the one shall be taken, and the other left."

13.   Luke 22:43--removed in the footnotes

14.   Luke 22:44--removed in the footnotes

15.   Luke 23:17--**COMPLETELY** removed [also deleted from the Jehovah's Witness "Bible"]. What are you NIV readers missing?   *"(For of necessity he must release one unto them at the feast.)"*

16.   John 5:4--**COMPLETELY** removed [also deleted from the Jehovah's Witness "Bible"]. What are you NIV readers missing? *"For an angel went down at a certain season into the pool, and troubled the water: whosoever then first after the troubling of the water stepped in was made whole of whatsoever disease he had."*

17.   John 7:53-8:11--removed in the footnotes

18.   Acts 8:37--**COMPLETELY** removed [also deleted from the Jehovah's Witness "Bible"]. It's deletion makes one think that people can be baptized and saved without believing on the Lord Jesus Christ. Sounds Catholic. What are you NIV readers missing?   *"And Philip said, If thou believest with all thine heart, thou mayest. And he answered and said, I believe that Jesus Christ is the Son of God."*

19.   Acts 15:34--**COMPLETELY** removed [also deleted from the Jehovah's Witness "Bible"]. What are you NIV readers missing? *"Notwithstanding it pleased Silas to abide there still."*

20.   Acts 24:7--**COMPLETELY** removed [also deleted from the Jehovah's Witness "Bible"]. What are you NIV readers missing? *"But the chief captain Lysias came upon us, and with great violence took him away out of our hands,"*

21.   Acts 28:29--**COMPLETELY** removed [also deleted from the Jehovah's Witness "Bible"]. What are you NIV readers missing? *"And when he had said these words, the Jews departed, and had great reasoning among themselves."*

22.   Romans 16:24--**COMPLETELY** removed [also deleted from the Jehovah's Witness "Bible"]. What are you NIV readers missing?   *"The grace of our Lord Jesus Christ be with you all. Amen."*

23.   I John 5:7--Vitally important phrase **COMPLETELY** removed [also deleted from the Jehovah's Witness "Bible"]. In the NIV it says, *"For there are three that testify:"*

Compare the NIV reading with the following Jehovah's Witness reading-- *"For there are three witness bearers,"*

What are you NIV readers missing? What does the real Bible say? *"For there are three that bear record in heaven, the Father, the Word, and the Holy Ghost: and these three are one."*

This is one of the GREATEST verses testifying of the Trinity. That is why the Jehovah's Witnesses leave it out. They do not believe in the Trinity and they do not believe that Jesus is God. Why does the NIV leave it out? Whole books have been written on the manuscript evidence that supports inclusion of this verse in the Bible. Reader, do you believe in the triunity of God? If so, then this deletion should offend you. People are playing around with the Bible and it isn't funny!

NIV Reader: Do you have enough confidence in the NIV to...tell God, OUT LOUD, that these verses do not belong in the Bible? If not, you need to get a King James so you can have some confidence.

One writer said to me, "You [do not] talk about the large section of Mark [referring to Mark 16:9-20] which was INCLUDED with the provision that the earliest reliable manuscripts did not include that section."

I said to him, That "provisional" statement is, at best, casting doubt on the word of God and at worst deleting the information in the footnotes. You say that the NIV says, the MOST RELIABLE manuscripts don't have it. That is as good as saying, "If you accept this rendering you are accepting an inferior, unreliable manuscript." What they DON'T tell you is that those same "reliable" manuscripts don't even include the whole book of Revelation!!! If the manuscript is so reliable, then why didn't they take out the whole book of Revelation? Selective deletion? Why not be true to what they say are the earliest and most reliable manuscripts? I have no respect for this.

This is a fight for the Words of God, the product of the Reformation, the Authorized King James Version of 1611.

What About The E.S.V.?

QUESTION #538

Does it seem to you that there is an explosion of references and links to the English Standard Version (ESV) as of late? What's going on? I did a little research and found that the ESV is based on the RSV which I guess went over like a lead balloon when it was first released. Why is the ESV so popular now and seemingly endorsed or used by so many prominent Bible teachers and commentators? Is it about money, or something more sinister? Are there any videos on your site which speak specifically to the ESV?

ANSWER #538

You are correct that the English Standard Version (ESV) has been boosted by many Fundamental schools such as Bob Jones University (BJU). It is sold in its bookstore and pushed by BJU, its graduates, and its friends without doubt.

I do not know the reason for this other than that it's a new version which has allegedly been revised by "*trustworthy*" people.

Like the apostate-produced Revised Standard Version (RSV) in the 1950's, the ESV New Testament is based entirely on the Gnostic Critical Greek words. These words have 8,000 differences when compared to the Words underlying the King James Bible (KJB). Among these more than 8,000 differences there are at least 356 doctrinal passages that are in error in the ESV just like they were in error in the apostate-edited RSV from which the ESV was revised. We have four-or five-articles exposing the details of the ESV. If you want to receive these articles, just e-mail me at BFT@BibleForToday.org, and I will e-mail you all of these without charge.

Getting A TR Japanese NT
QUESTION #539

I wondered if you could help me locate a Japanese Bible or NT following the Traditional Text. I tried Bearing Precious Seed but it does not know of any.

ANSWER #539

There is a Japanese translation that is supposed to be a good one, but the head of the mission agency that sponsors the Japanese missionary doing the translation forbade him from communicating to me about it. This mission leader claims he is angry with me for a statement I made about Dr. Ernest Pickering (a Dallas Theological Seminary classmate of mine). It is a ridiculous reason for failure to cooperate with me and other Christians about the Japanese Bible. This mission leader said he would come and talk to me about it when in the area, but he has never come. It has been about two years since his promise.

Omitting Words From The Bible
QUESTION #540

I was listening to the debate between yourself and James White on the radio over the issue of KJB and other versions. I heard you mention that some translators are trained to take out parts that come up more than once. I can't remember exactly what you said. Do you have any information on this? Can you prove it to be true for subtractions in a particular example?

ANSWER #540

There is a book designed and used by Bible translators. In this book, it tells the translators how to handle what is called "*implicit*" information or that which is "*implied*" in their minds. If the translator thinks it is implied, he can add it to the Words of God. This is sin.

The translator's book also tells the translators how to handle "*explicit*" information or things which are explicitly and clearly written in the Bible, but which might be duplicated in some way and by some words. If this is the case, the translator can remove any such duplicated words of the Bible. This is the way many new versions treat "*explicit information.*"

If something is repeated twice or more, the book suggests that the translator need only to include it one time, and remove the duplication. Below is an example.

Luke 8:35-38 "*Then they went out to see what was done; and came to Jesus, and found the man, **out of whom the devils were departed**, sitting at the feet of Jesus, clothed, and in his right mind: and they were afraid. They also which saw it told them by what means **he that was possessed of the devils** was healed. Then the whole multitude of the country of the Gadarenes round about besought him to depart from them; for they were taken with great fear: and he went up into the ship, and returned back again. Now the man **out of whom the devils were departed** besought him that he might be with him: but Jesus sent him away, saying,*"

You'll notice that in three different places the Bible teaches that this man had "*devils*" within him. According to this translation book, the translator would be free to omit two of the three references to the having "*devils*" within him. Other examples could also be given. This is a sinful and a wicked way of handling the very Words of the Living God! Yet, along with the way modern versions handle "*implicit*" information, this is the way many handle even "*explicit*" information.

Refuting ESV And NASV

QUESTION #541

I have been studying this topic since I found the Lord Jesus Christ ten years ago. Most of my friends like the ESV and NASB. I am not a preacher, but went to seminary. My professors told me that the KJV has gone through hundreds of revisions, and that some of the texts were doctored to make it more readable. I struggle some with this issue because it is difficult to sift through all of the emotional sales rhetoric, and get down to the facts. I would like to find some good actual sources for the accusations that are made in your articles and documents. If you have some, I would be grateful.

ANSWER #541

I would suggest you get my book, *Defending The King James Bible* (**BFT #1594** @ **$12.00 + $7.00 S&H**). You can order with credit card by phone at 856-854-4452 or online as **BFT #1594** on our website (BibleForToday.org) and then go to our BFT Web Store and put in #1594. In the Appendix, I have over 1,000 other titles defending the King James Bible and its underlying Hebrew, Aramaic, and Greek Words.

CHAPTER VI

QUESTIONS ABOUT THE

KING JAMES BIBLE

The 1769 King James Bible
QUESTION #542

We recently received the *Defined King James Bible* and are taking orders for more. The title page says "*Cambridge 1769 Text.*" Documentation that I've read shows Dr. Blayney's 1769 edition as Oxford. Could you explain the difference?

ANSWER #542

The 1769 King James Bible text was published by both Cambridge and Oxford. Cambridge did a more accurate job of this. This is why we have used the "*Cambridge 1769 Text*" rather than the Oxford.

No Translation Mistakes
QUESTION #543

You made a statement that you believed there were no mistakes in the KJV. Could you explain what this means in more detail? Did you mean the KJV is inerrant? I thought only the Scriptures given by inspiration were inerrant, because only inspired words can be without error. I have a *Defined King James Bible* that I bought from Condell Park Bible Church in Sydney. I understand you know Pastor Brian Wenham who has made a great stand for Christ in our country and he stands boldly for the King James Bible. My pastor has a copy of your book *Defending the King James Bible* which I will read as soon as I can borrow it. Finally could you recommend a short list of books that our church could purchase that would help us understand this vital issue.

ANSWER #543

I have said many times that I have not found any "*translational mistakes*" in the King James Bible. (1) Though they could have used other meanings, I believe they used at least one of the five or six legitimate meanings of the

Hebrew, Aramaic, or Greek Words. (2) Though they could have used other rules, I believe they used at least one of the legitimate rules of syntax or grammar for Hebrew, Aramaic, and Greek.

While others do not see eye to eye with me on this, I do not use the words *"inerrant, infallible, or perfect"* for our KJB. These are terms that Ruckmanites and others use for the KJB. I want to be far removed from Ruckman's vocabulary whenever possible. I reserve these words for the preserved, inerrant, infallible, perfect and inspired Hebrew, Aramaic, and Greek Words underlying the King James Bible.

Of the over 1,000 books we carry defending the KJB and its underlying Hebrew, Aramaic, and Greek Words, I will attach a list of only 83 titles (which is still far too long a list) which you can look over and then, perhaps you can narrow it down to 5 or 10 and then you can ask me about them and I can suggest ones I would recommend. Let me suggest a few you might consider to get a good background on this by BFT ##: #83, #595, #611, #1131, #1428, #1594, #2423; #2671, #2777, #2928, #2956, #2974, #2987, #3010, #3064BK, #3125, #3138, #3195, #3230, #3234, #3259, #3302, #3308, #3344, #3345, #3350DVD, #3375, #3386, #3392, & #3426. These are 30 of the 1,000 available. You must decide which you should get for your church library.

Though I don't know Pastor Brian Wenham personally, we carry one of the books he co-authored on *Jesus And Divorce--No Remarriage Until Mate's Death.*

The "Pure" Cambridge Text?
QUESTION #544

I have recently found a website www.bibleprotector.com. These young ministers are saying that the 1769 Cambridge Text is not the Pure Cambridge Edition. They say that the 1769 Cambridge Text is based on the Concord Edition Text. Is that true and could you explain?

ANSWER #544

So far as I know the Cambridge Press edition used in our *Defined King James Bible* is unchanged from 1769. I am not inclined to trust these denials made by this website. I would like to see some of their so-called changes before I am convinced they are correct.

Indispensable King James Bible
QUESTION #545

I have been using my Bible For Today, a black leather bound KJV Bible for quite some time, and have found it to be indispensable in my walk as a follower of Christ.   I do believe that the KJV Bible is the most superior translation of the Scriptures.

On the Internet on some other KJV-only sites, however, I have seen people advocating a position that all other non-KJV Bibles are "*counterfeit*." Although I haven't seen this phrase on the BibleForToday.org website, these claims on the other sites leave me with some questions that I was wondering if you could shed some light on. If you could please send me your input to these questions at your earliest convenience it would be much appreciated.

ANSWER #545

Thanks for your note. I am glad the *Defined King James Bible* is helpful.

As to the use the word, "*counterfeit*" for non-KJB Bibles, the definitions below seem to fit most if not all of them.

counterfeit

adjective

1   made in imitation of something genuine so as to deceive or defraud; forged (counterfeit money)

2   pretended; sham; feigned (counterfeit sorrow)

noun

1   a) an imitation made to deceive; forgery b) something that so closely resembles something else as to mislead

2   (Obs.) an impostor; cheat

transitive verb, intransitive verb

1   to make an imitation of (money, pictures, etc.), usually in order to deceive or defraud

2   to pretend; feign

3   to resemble (something) closely

SYN. false, artificial

noun

Etymology

(ME countrefete derived from OFr contrefait, pp. of contrefaire, to make in opposition, imitate derived from contre-, counter- + faire derived from L facere, to make, do1)

A KJB Reformed Seminary
QUESTION #546

I have spent three years in Mexico doing missionary work. But now upon returning to the United States I have the desire to study in a seminary in order to learn Greek and Hebrew. But I am having problems finding a seminary that shares my beliefs (Calvinistic or Reformed Baptist) and that holds to the KJV of the Bible. If you could help me with this I would be forever indebted to you. Your web site has helped me so much and I thank God for you.

ANSWER #546

Though I am not of the Reformed Baptist position, it is very difficult to get the KJB and Calvinism and Reformed Baptist together. The only school I know of in this country that does this would be the Puritan Reformed Theological Seminary where Dr. Joel R. Beeke is President and professor of Systematic Theology and Homiletics. He is also the pastor of the Heritage Netherlands Reformed Congregation of Grand Rapids, Michigan.

He has a tract called "Practical Reasons For Retaining The KJB." It is put out by Banner of Truth Tract Mission at 540 Crescent St., N.E., Grand Rapids, MI. 49503.

Dr. Beeke's phones are: 616-285-8102 for Residence and Office: 616-977-0599 Ext. 123. You can ask him about Greek and Hebrew studies in his seminary.

Though we're not "*reformed*," I do teach a 1st and 2nd year Greek course and a 1st year Hebrew course on MP-3 disks that are available if you choose to go that way. I am glad that our Internet ministry is helpful for you.

King James Study Bible?
QUESTION #547

I have enjoyed listening to many of your KJV Defense messages on-line, and appreciate your presentations. I think we should make up a King James Study Bible. Is this a project you think you could identify with?

ANSWER #547

Your thought of a KJB Study Bible is interesting. Do you have available the $30,000 to $50,000 ++ in order to print it once you have it written? Unless you have the funds, I personally think it is a "*pipe dream*" as we say.

The Cambridge 1769 KJB
QUESTION #548

I just had a person email me the following link.
http://www.biblebelievers.com/believers-org/counterfeit-kjv.HTMl
I really needed to get your take on this as they recommend the Bibles at:
Bearing Precious Seed Ministries
 See: http://www.bpsmilford.org/store.html

I always recommend your Bibles, but are these all right to recommend to someone that just wants a KJV (text only)?

And if what they are saying is true about the new Cambridge Bibles, are only your Bibles (and the Bibles at the above link) the only ones left keeping to the preserved Word of God?

ANSWER #548

I do not have information on the King James Bibles offered at Bearing Precious Seed Ministries, one way or another.

Our *Defined King James Bible* is a Cambridge 1769 text. It has not changed any of the words mentioned in the LINK above. Here are a few samples of 1769 words that are still there in our Bible.
1. "asswaged" is there
2. "basons" is still there.
3. "chesnut" is still there.
4. "cloke" is still there
    From this partial sampling, I would conclude that our 1769 Cambridge text is sound and genuine. The LINK above might be referring to the Oxford text that changes many spellings. It also would refer to King James Bibles published by other USA Bible publishers such as Moody, Zondervan, Nelson, and others that change many spellings. "*Esaias*" is changed to "*Isaiah*." "*Elias*" is changed to "*Elijah*," and so forth.

"*God Forbid*"
QUESTION #549

I am debating the KJV Bible with a 20-year old so-called Greek scholar that attacks the KJV Bible. Since I do not know or read Greek he says that the words, "*God forbid*," in Romans 6:2 should have been in italics in the KJV Bible because "*God*" is not in the Textus Receptus at Romans 6:2. How should I answer him?

ANSWER #549

First of all, I wouldn't waste time talking with a person who really doesn't want to learn, but only wants to argue against the KJB.

Second, the expression "*God forbid*" is a translation of ME GENOITO which is literally "*may it never come to pass.*" In 1611, and even today, the expression "*God forbid*" expresses these words accurately.

New Translation For Today?
QUESTION #550

I do believe the Words of the Textus Receptus are the true inspired Words of God. I believe the King James Version is a true translation of those Words. But I have a hard time accepting that the Words of God could not now be accurately translated today in modern English. Many of our churches have embraced faulty translations because they are in modern English. I fear we will lose more if we cannot find some godly scholars who believe in the veracity of the inspired Words who will provide a solid translation for our day and time. We who believe the King James Bible have not provided a new, true translation in our era. Have we held too tenaciously to the old? Maybe some of us are afraid of being branded a heretick if we advocate such a thing. What do you think?

ANSWER #550

What you say is indeed "*possible*," but it is not "*probable*" due to (1) a total lack of men any where nearly as qualified as the KJB translators; (2) lack of skilled men who hold to the Hebrew, Aramaic, and Greek Words underlying the KJB; (3) lack of qualified men to use only verbal and formal equivalence translation techniques; (4) lack of publishers that will publish a sound translation found only upon the Traditional Hebrew, Aramaic, and Greek Words underlying the King James Bible.

Is The *Defined KJB* Cambridge?
QUESTION #551

Do you sell Cambridge Bibles? Is your *Defined King James Bible* a Cambridge Bible?

ANSWER #551

The only Bible we sell is a Cambridge Bible. It is called the *Defined King James Bible.*

Dr. Floyd Nolan Jones
QUESTION #552

Someone just recently told me of a man named Dr. Floyd Nolan Jones who writes on the authority of the Bible. Do you know of this man? Is he of like faith & belief in the TR? Or is he more in the camp of Peter Ruckman?

ANSWER #552

From the books that I have read of him, from writing to him, from talking with him from time to time, and publishing several of his books, I found him to be sound, scholarly, and in accord with my own position on the King James Bible and its underlying Hebrew, Aramaic, and Greek Words. Dr. Jones is most definitely not a follower of Peter Ruckman.

Discrepancies In The KJB Bible?
QUESTION #553

Thank you for your correct stand on the King James Bible. I have run across a book called *Toward a Mature Faith: Does Biblical Inerrancy Make Sense?* by Clayton Sullivan. He gives allegedly 200 discrepancies in the Bible. I have solved some of them, but I am wondering if you have any material that has dealt with most of these discrepancy issues.

ANSWER #553

Regarding so-called Bible difficulties, I have always recommended a book by a Bible-believing astronomer who used to work at Baldwin Wallace College in Berea, Ohio where I went to High School. He retired in July, 2007 from that school. His name is Dr. Gerardus Bowe. The title of his 265-page book is *The Book of Bible Problems*.

Another book which I have is by Dr. Chester Kulas entitled *Those So-Called Errors*. It is 430 pages in length and can be purchased by calling 1-603-632-7408. I hope your friend can find one of these two books which will help him in the so-called errors.

Content Of KJB Seminar #10
QUESTION #554

Going back to your most recent KJB Seminar #10 given at the Fairhaven Baptist College a few years ago, what are the contents and information in that 4-video set? I'm assuming it is very in-depth.

ANSWER #554

In this full King James Bible Seminar I quote from about 35 books including those five by Dean John W. Burgon. It was a four day series of seven class hours per day, for a total of 28 class hours. It is my Power Point presentations with class discussion as well. It covers the KJB's superior texts of Hebrew, Aramaic, and Greek, superior translators, superior translation technique, and superior theology.

Videos Defending The KJB

QUESTION #555

I plan to order this in the near future. Should I remind you via e-mail about the recent DVDs being the desired set when I'm about to order? What are the contents of the recent video presentations? Do they include manuscript evidence? Also, which is your most concise video on KJB defense (time & information wise)?

ANSWER #555

You can e-mail your order at BFT@BibleForToday.org or call our phone at 856-854-4452 with your credit card. The videos include some manuscript evidence, though it would be impossible to present it all. The following item is a condensed video of one of my presentations in defense of the King James Bible and its underlying Hebrew. Aramaic, and Greek Words.

2516VCR $15.00+$7.00 S&H KJB Seminar in VA Local Church--Four-Fold Superiority Waite, Dr. D. A.

This is a condensed VHS video on this theme. It is 6 hours or less. The KJB Seminar presents four reasons for KJB superiority including Texts, Translators, Technique, and Theology. You can order these online, or by mail.

Definitive KJB Video?

QUESTION #556

I have another question for you brother: What is your most definitive video cassette or series on the defense of the King James Bible? I see your website, biblefortoday.org offers several videos on this subject.

ANSWER #556

My most definitive DVD in defense of the KJB is my KJB Seminar #10 given at the Fairhaven Baptist College a few years ago. It is four days, seven hours per day. It is in 4 DVD's for a gift of $45.00 + $7.00 S&H. Just order it by KJB Seminar #10 and we'll know what you mean.

Defined KJB--Sewn Or Glued?

QUESTION #557

I'm looking for a good quality Bible with a wide margin. It seems I may have found it here. Do your *Defined King James Bibles* have a sewn or glued binding? The description on your web page doesn't say.

ANSWER #557

All of our *Defined King James Bibles* are Smyth sewn. They are not glued.

Talking To Misguided Seminarians
QUESTION #558

Pastor Waite, will you be able to talk to the misguided Seminarians and give them some background about the different versions of the Bible? Probably conducting seminars to introduce the *Defined King James Bible*? Probably, you already have done that or thought about it.

ANSWER #558

I am always willing to speak to students at any college or seminary, but the invitations do not come in. They have a negative attitude against those of us who stand for the Textus Receptus and the KJB. Many of them smear us as being followers of Peter Ruckman (which is completely false). These schools are steeled in their false views of the Greek New Testament and even the Hebrew Old Testament. We need to pray for those few schools, colleges, and seminaries that teach soundly in these matters.

Differences In King James Bibles
QUESTION #559

The *Defined King James Bible* is an excellent Bible and I do appreciate it so much. The cover page says that the *Defined King James Bible* is the Cambridge 1769 text. What would be the criteria for determining, for instance, whether the Old Scofield (1917) or the Thompson Chain Reference Bible, was the 1769 Cambridge text? Is there some mark, or some way to identify whether a text in one of these Bibles is the 1769 Cambridge text?

ANSWER #559

We know that our *Defined King James Bible* is the Cambridge 1769 because that is the one we used in it. I know that the Old Scofield states it is by the Oxford University Press instead of Cambridge. Perhaps the Thompson Chain Bible also prints its origin on the title page. Other than that, unless it is either Oxford or Cambridge from England(which have a kind of copyright), most King James Bibles printed in the USA have changed many spellings and are neither Oxford nor Cambridge. Cambridge is far superior in exactness to Oxford which has many differences from the original.

These strange alleged King James Bibles are published by Zondervan, Moody, Kregel, and other U.S. publishers. The way to detect these false and phony KJB's is to look up the spelling of such words as Esaias (they put Isaiah), Elias (they put Elijah), Jeremy (they put Jeremiah), and Jesus (in certain places, they have Joshua), etc.

The KJB's Superior Foundation

QUESTION #560

I've been reading through your latest book *The Superior Foundation of the King James Bible* (**BFT #3384** @ **$10.00 + $7.00 S&H**). You've done well in presenting things. I have a couple of questions.

On page 34, I don't understand what is meant that there are "*other Traditional Received Texts*" and that Scrivener's is the most accurate. What are the other Traditional Received texts? Why is Scrivener's considered most accurate? I would think it would either be totally accurate or not. I'm not sure what is meant.

On page 33, I don't understand why the KJB editors departed from the Beza 5th edition in favor of 8 other sources. Did the other Bibles previous to the KJB not use those 8 other sources? What was wrong with the Beza 5th edition in those areas that they went to the 8 other sources? What were the changes that were made?

ANSWER #560

I'm glad you're reading *The Superior Foundation of the King James Bible*.

1. Other "*traditional texts*" include those of Erasmus, the Complutensian Polyglot, Stephens, and Elzevir. I believe the Beza's 5th edition, 1598, is the "*most accurate*," having gone through 82 years of refinements from 1516 to 1598. I believe, personally, through both the facts involved and my faith, that it is not only the "*most accurate*" compared with the others, but that this Greek Text is a copy of the original Greek New Testament.

2. The KJB translators, for their own wise reasons, departed from Beza's 5th in only 190 places which is a minor number considering there are over 140,000 Words in the Greek N.T.

KJB In Modern English Possible?

QUESTION #561

Is it possible to translate the Bible from the "*correct original language Bible Texts*" to modern English of today? The young people at our church are stuck with a poor translation because the pastor here will not use the King James Bible and there are none that are based on and use the correct original texts underlying the King James Bible and are presented in modern English that is true to the original languages. Are we stuck with an out-dated use of the English language when we want to read the Bible in English?

ANSWER 561

The project you mention is "*possible*," but I don't think it is "*probable*" that it will be done in the near or far future for the following reasons:

1.   There is a problem of finding modern-day translators who are thoroughly equipped in the languages of Hebrew, Aramaic, Greek, and English.

2.   There is a problem of finding the above translators who also are totally committed to the Hebrew, Aramaic, and Greek Words underlying the KJB rather than the Gnostic Critical Greek Text and an improper Old Testament Text.

3.   There is a problem of finding a publisher that will print such a Bible since publishers have been turned off of the TR and Masoretic Hebrew. Some will not publish any books that use the King James Bible and the Words that underlie it.

4.   There is a problem of finding $50,000 to $100.000 or more to print even a few thousand such Bibles.

5.   There is a problem of finding bookstores and outlets that will carry such a Bible. Most of them sell other versions based on false foundations.

6.   There is a problem of finding pastors and people who would buy such a Bible since they have been programed to turn from it.

7.   If you can solve all six of these problems, be my guest in solving the problems.

8.   In the meantime, I suggest that everyone should get a copy of our *Defined King James Bible* which gives meanings of uncommon words. This will allow people to understand the King James Bible clearly without the need to make another English Bible. The old adage is still true, "*If it isn't broken, why fix it?*"

KJB And The Latin Vulgate
QUESTION #562

As you know we are embroiled in the Spanish Bible controversy down here in Chile. One of the accusations thrown at us has to do with the KJV. They have stated that the KJV follows the Latin Vulgate and not the TR in "*more than 60 places.*" I find this completely preposterous, but I thought I would run it by you and ask your opinion on it. I did run across Dr. Edward Hills' statement that the KJV seems to follow the Vulgate in Luke 23:42. However, on further analysis Hills states that the KJV clearly follows earlier English versions. So, is there any single place where the KJV follows the Latin Vulgate to the exclusion of all other sources?

ANSWER #562

I think Dr. Hills stated that in about 7 or 8 places, the Latin Vulgate was followed, though other English versions might have also been used. I would agree with you in doubting that there are "*more than 60 places*" where this took place. Dr. Hills looked into this very carefully in his book, *The King James Bible Defended* (**BFT #0084** @ **$18.00** + **$7.00 S&H**).

Dr. *Scrivener's Annotated Greek New Testament* (**BFT #1670** @ **$35.00** + **$7.00 S&H**) lists only 190 places in all in the APPENDIX where Beza's 5th Edition, 1598, was not followed. Most of these sources were from other Greek sources, not the Latin Vulgate. You can check them over yourself if you wish. You might ask this person to send you the more than "*60 places*" that have followed the Latin Vulgate rather than the Greek Text. I would be very glad to check out every one of them to see where the Greek Words were not followed.

What About The KJB's Apocrypha

ANSWER #563

I heard some researcher mentioned that if you have a KJV (1885 or prior) that it included the book of II Maccabees (and I am assuming I Maccabees). I do not believe him but I thought I should get your take on this.

ANSWER #563

The entire Apocrypha, including 1 and 2 Maccabees) was included in the AV 1611, but I do not know positively when it was removed. Some say 15 years or 25 years. I certainly do not believe they kept it until 1885. That is way too long to have it in the KJB.

It should never have been included in the original King James Bible. It is filled with errors and contradictions with the genuine Bible. Without going into the Apocrypha in detail, I have found the following LINK to be helpful: http://www.jesus-is-lord.com/apocryph.htm. If you want to look into the Apocrypha further, you can study it there. It will tell you why the Apocrypha is not in the King James Bible today and therefore why it should not have been there in 1611 when it was first published.

Six Questions To Decide

QUESTION #564

Please could you confirm which of the following statements is right and recommend reading to prove it.

1a When the KJV was translated, they only really had Byzantine texts to work from.

1b When the KJV was translated, they had plenty of text types available but chose to reject those that followed the Critical Text.

2a Erasmus imported readings straight from the Vulgate.

2b Erasmus never imported readings from the Vulgate.

3a Sheol and Hades simply mean "*realm of the dead*" not "*Hell.*"

3b Sheol and Hades can mean "Hell" depending on the context.

4a In 2Timothy 3:17, the correct term is "*equipping*"
"*That the man of God may be **perfect**, throughly furnished unto all good works.*"

4b In 2Timothy 3:17, The Greek word means "*perfect*". The word "*complete*" is used elsewhere in the KJV proving the translators decided it was inappropriate here.

5a Every papyrus manuscript is Alexandrian.

5b There are an amazing number of Byzantine readings in the papyrus manuscripts.

6a Early translations of the NT were from Alexandrian manuscripts.

6b The above (6a) cannot be proven.

ANSWER #564

1b is correct.

2b is correct. Some say Erasmus used the last 6 verses of the Latin Vulgate for Revelation, but even others say he had Greek MSS even for those verses.

3b is correct. Sheol and Hades are mere letter-for-letter "*transliterations*" and not "*translations*" of these Hebrew and Greek Words.

4b is correct. The Greek word, ARTIOS, has many meanings. "*Perfect*" is one of them.

5b is correct. According to the research of Dr. Jack Moorman in *Forever Settled* (**BFT #1428 @ $20.00 + $7.00 S&H**), and, as mentioned on page 56 of my book, *Defending the King James Bible* (**BFT #1594 @ $12.00 + $7.00 S&H**), of the 88 papyrus MSS as of 1967, 13 were from the Gnostic Critical Greek Text and 75 were from the Traditional Greek Text (That is 15% vs. 85%).

6b is correct. In fact, the evidence of Mark 16:9-20 (as found in the multitude of MSS, the early versions prior to 4th century, and in the quotations and allusions of the church fathers prior to the 4th century) proves that these verses were in the original Gospel of Mark. It proves that they were cut out of the 4th century Vatican and Sinai MSS due to some editor's whim. Other examples can also be given to prove that the original New Testament consisted of the Traditional Text Greek Words underlying the KJB, and that the Alexandrian Vatican and Sinai MSS were corruptions made by the Gnostic heretics whose headquarters were in Alexandria, Egypt. These corruptions were made to further their heretical teachings.

As I told you on the phone. Dr. Jack Moorman's *Forever Settled* (**BFT #1428 @ $20.00 + $7.00 S&H**) and Dr. H. D. Williams' *The Lie That Changed the Modern World* (**BFT #3125 @ $16.00 + $7.00 S&H**) are two good books that will give you much background and material on these various subjects you have asked about.

KJV 1611 & Peter Ruckman
QUESTION #565
I have a two-fold question: (1) I have a 1611 KJV and an old Scofield Bible and compare the two, except for old English spellings, I have not noticed much difference in doctrine, etc; have I missed something? Are you a group that only approves of the 1611 KJV? (2)Secondly, what is your opinion of Peter S. Ruckman's writings?

ANSWER #565
1.   The AV 1611 is fairly similar to our present KJB's. There are thousands of spellings and punctuation differences, but only between 400 to 1,000 small adding of words or changing words that do not change the sense. No doctrine is involved that I have seen.

2.   In my considered opinion, I think Peter S. Ruckman's writings (and those of his follower, Gail Riplinger) are as dangerous to the honest and proper King James Bible cause as are the Gnostic Critical Greek Text writings. I say this because his (and her) wild ideas (for example, saying the KJB is inspired of God and corrects even the Hebrew and Greek from which it was taken) are linked to my ideas and others of us who have a sound and sane position defending the King James Bible. We are then dismissed as Ruckmanites (or Riplingerites) and our views are discarded along with his. We are repeatedly called Ruckmanites (or Riplingerites) because we defend both our KJB and the preserved original Hebrew, Aramaic, and Greek Words that underlie it.

"Baptism" Or "Immersion"?
QUESTION #566
How do those who are "KJV Only" answer why the word, "*baptism,*" was never translated "*immersion*"? Could it be that those who do the translating are more interested in the money than accuracy or preferences?

ANSWER #566
I don't know why the KJB translators didn't make BAPTO or BAPTIZO as "*immerse.*" They merely transliterated it (that is, letter-for-letter) and let the interpretation be for those who read the word. They did not actually "*translate*"

it.

CHAPTER VII

QUESTIONS ABOUT OLD

TESTAMENT WORD

MEANINGS

Meaning Of "Kill" In Exodus 20:13

QUESTION #567

A minister friend of mine said that the King James translation was wrong in Exodus 20:13 when using the word "*kill*." Could you help me?

Thanks for your book, *Defending The King James Bible*. I keep copies to hand to those who want to know the Truth!

ANSWER #567

Here is what one Hebrew Lexicon has to say concerning the meaning of the Hebrew Word used in this verse:

07523 **ratsach** {raw-tsakh'}

a primitive root; TWOT - 2208; v

AV - slayer 16, murderer 14, kill 5, murder 3, slain 3, manslayer 2,
   killing 1, slayer + 0310 1, slayeth 1, death 1; 47

1) **to murder**, slay, kill

 1a) (Qal) **to murder**, slay

  1a1) premeditated

  1a2) accidental

  1a3) as avenger

  1a4) slayer (intentional) (participle)

 1b) (Niphal) to be slain

 1c) (Piel)

  1c1) **to murder**, assassinate

  1c2) murderer, assassin (participle)(subst)

 1d) (Pual) to be killed

I believe the primary meaning of "*kill*" in this Hebrew Word to "*kill by murder*" and not "*kill*" in the sense of the government using capital punishment for those who commit first-degree murder. This is the same Hebrew word used in Numbers 35:16-21 for the "*murderer*" who is to be "*put to death.*"

Numbers 35:16-21 *And if he smite him with an instrument of iron, so that he die, he is a murderer: the murderer shall surely be put to death.*
17 And if he smite him with throwing a stone, wherewith he may die, and he die, he is a murderer: the murderer shall surely be put to death.
18 Or if he smite him with an hand weapon of wood, wherewith he may die, and he die, he is a murderer: the murderer shall surely be put to death.
19 The revenger of blood himself shall slay the murderer: when he meeteth him, he shall slay him.
20 But if he thrust him of hatred, or hurl at him by laying of wait, that he die;
21 Or in enmity smite him with his hand, that he die: he that smote him shall surely be put to death; for he is a murderer. The revenger of blood shall slay the murderer, when he meeteth him.

These verses show clearly that capital punishment for first degree murderers is Biblical and is required. That is not "*killing*" in the sense of Exodus 20:13. The English word, "*kill*," has many meanings, and it is used correctly in one of its meaning in Exodus 20:13.

Here are the first two meanings and usages of "*kill*" from the *Oxford English Dictionary*. You notice meaning #2d has a special meaning which includes "to commit murder." I think this is the sense of the KJB's use of it in the commandment, "*Thou shalt not kill*" (Exodus 20:13).
d. *absol.* To perform the act of killing; to commit murder or slaughter.
kill (kĬl), *v.* Pa. tense and pple. killed (kĬld). Forms: a. 3-4 culle(n, kulle(n(ü).
b. 4 kille(n, 4-5 kylle, 6 kyll, 6-7 kil, 6- kill. c. 5-6 kelle. d. *Sc.* 5-6 kele, keill.
pa. tense 3-4 culde, 4-6 kild(e, 5 kyld(e, (5-6 kelit, etc.); 4- killed. *pa.* pple. 4
(y-)culled, (i-)kilde), y-keld, 4- killed (5-6 kyld, kelyt, keild, etc., 6 kylt, 6-
kilt).
[Of obscure origin; not found in the cognate langs.
If in OE., its type would be *cyllan*, conjecturally referred to an OTeut. *kuljan*,
ablaut-variant of *kwaljan*, whence OE. *cwellan* to quell; but the original sense
is against this. Known first in Layamon, and in southern texts, in form *cüllen*,
küllen. In midl. dial. normally *kille(n, kill*, the common form in ME.; *kelle* is
rare. The usual Sc. form in 15-16th c. was *kele, keill*, the vowel of which is
difficult to account for. In ME. the pa. tense and pa. pple. varied between *killed*
and *kild*; exceptionally the pple. appears as *kilt* (cf. *spilt*), now regarded as an
Irishism, and sometimes used jocularly, esp. in sense 6 b.]
† 1. a. *trans.* To stirke, hit; to beat, knock. Also with *off*, and *absol. or intr.*

Also *fig. Obs.*

c1205 Lay. 20319 Ofte me hine smæt mid smærte Šerden; ofte me hine culde; swa me deð crosce.

a1225 *Ancr. R.* 126 þauh a word culle Þe [= thee] ful herde up o Þine heorte.

13.. *E.E. Allit. P.* B. 876 We kylle of Þyn heued.

a1375 *Joseph Arim.* 545 He starte vp and streiŠte to his hache, culles on mennes hedes Þat Þei doun lyen.

† b. To cast or throw *out*; to clear *out*.

(For a similar connexion between the notions of striking and throwing, cf. the senses of G. *schlagen* (Da. *slaa*) slay, and *schmeissen* (Da. *smide*) smite.)

a1225 *Ancr. R.* 346 Auh to hire owune schrift-feder, oðer to summe oðre lif-holie monne: ¼if heo mei hine habben, kulle al ut Þet is iðe krocke [*v.r.* culle al Þe pot ut].

2. a. To put to death; to deprive of life; to slay, slaughter. In early use implying personal agency and the use of a weapon; later, extended to any means or cause which puts an end to life, as an accident, over-work, grief, drink, a disease, etc.

a.**c1330** *King of Tars* 179 The Sarazins withouten fayle The Cristene culde in that batayle.

13.. *Song Yesterday* 146 in *E.E.P.* (1862) 137 „if Þi neiŠebor Þe manas, OÞur to culle, oÞur to bete.

1377 Langl. *P. Pl.* B. Prol. 185 ThouŠ we culled [*C-text* 199 hadde ycullid] Þe catte, Šut sholde Þer come another.

Ibid. xvi. 137 Thei casten & contreueden To kulle hym whan Þei miŠte.

b.**c1374** Chaucer *Anel. & Arc.* 53 Yche other for to kylle With blody speris.

1382 Wyclif *Luke* xx. 15 This is the eyr, sle we him... And thei killiden him.

1387 Trevisa *Higden* (Rolls) VIII. 5 At Wycombmalban Þey were i-kilde [*v.r.* y-keld].

c1400 *Destr. Troy* 1343 þaire kyng was kylt.

1538 Starkey *England* i. iii. 98 Commynly they be other kyld where they are brede or sold.

1590 Spenser *F.Q.* i. v. 26 What art thou, that telst of Nephews kilt?

1632 Lithgow *Trav.* x. 479 Men are rather killed with the impatience they have in adversity, then adversity it selfe.

1697 Dryden *Virg. Georg.* iv. 758 Orpheus..Whom ev'n the savage Beasts had spar'd, they kill'd, And strew'd his mangled Limbs about the Field.

1774 Goldsm. *Nat. Hist.* (1776) I. 358 This terrible blast..instantly kills all those that it involves in its passage.

1848 Thackeray *Van. Fair* xlv, He was killing himself by late hours and intense application.

1895 *Law Times* C. 133/2 A man who had been killed at a level crossing by a railway train.

fig.

1614 A. Saul *Game Chesse* A iv b, But as they [pawns] march who so they finde doe in their colour stand, Such may they kill.

c.**1387** [see b].

a1400 *Octouian* 1063 Thy fader hath keld Well many a bole and doun yfeld.

c1440 *Partonope* 1054 Kelle these peuple of fals lawe.

15.. in *Bann. MS.* If. 145 a, Telyeouris ar tyrranis in kelling of lyiss.

d.**c1470** Henry *Wallace* vi. 651 His brothir Hew was kelyt thar full cald.

1508 Kennedie *Flyting w. Dunbar* 271 The feild, Quhair twelve thowsand trew Scottismen wer keild.

1572 *Satir. Poems Reform.* xxxiii. 46 Sair boistit thay my husband commoun-weill, And maid thair vowis and aithis him for to keill.

a1605 Montgomerie *Misc. Poems* lii. 29 Vncourtesly thus keill thay mo Than I.

b. With adverbial extensions, as *kill out (away, †down, †up)*, *kill off*, to cut off completely, to remove, extinguish, or get rid of (a number, a whole tribe, etc.) by killing.

a1400-50 *Alexander* 2377 þe kyng of þaire kythe was killid doun & heded.

c1450 Holland *Howlat* 566 He..Kelit dovne thar capitanis.

1530 Palsgr. 598/2, I kyll up, as one that kylleth the resydewe where many have ben kylled afore.

1607 Topsell *Four-f. Beasts* (1658) 520 Although the fœcundity of Swine be great, yet it is better to kill off two or three,..then to permit them to suck their dam.

1641 Hinde *J. Bruen* xiv. 47 Hee presently killed up the game, and disparked the Parke.

1849 *Tait's Mag.* XVI. 90/1 The wars of the Roses killed them out.

1876 Tennyson *Queen Mary* iii. v, Sometimes I have wish'd That I were caught, and kill'd away at once Out of the flutter.

1894 H. Drummond *Ascent Man* 264 [Nature] produces fitness by killing off the unfit.

1966 R. M. Lockley *Grey Seal, Common Seal* x. 147 In New Zealand I saw how the red deer are killing out the young native forest trees in the South Island Alps.

1970 *New Scientist* 31 Dec. 576/1 Broilers are 'killed out' at eight weeks.

1972 *Country Life* 30 Nov. 1504/2 These small birds [*sc.* turkeys]..are killed out at 10-12 weeks of age.

c. With complement expressing the result: *to kill to (†into, unto) death*, *to kill dead*. (Cf. Ger. *todtschlagen*, Du. *doodslaan*.)

1362 Langl. *P. Pl.* A. xi. 282 Poule þe apostil þat no pite ne hadde, Cristene kynde to kille to deþe.

c1400 *Destr. Troy* 1734 The Grekes..kyld all our kynnesmen into colde dethe.

1614 Bp. Hall *No Peace with Rome* 21 (L.) In the popish churches..their very walls kill us dead.

1670 Cotton *Espernon* i. 1. 35 Some of the company..found the Horse..kill'd stone dead.

1700 Farquhar *Constant Couple* iv. ii, Are you sure you killed him dead?

1882 J. C. Morison *Macaulay* iii. 92 Bentley did kill his adversary dead.

d. *absol.* To perform the act of killing; to commit murder or slaughter.

1535 Coverdale *Exod.* xx. 13 Thou shalt not kyll.

1593 Shakes. *2 Hen. VI*, iv. iii. 8 Thou shalt haue a License to kill for a hundred lacking one.

1653 Holcroft *Procopius, Pers. Wars* i. 2 Which gives such force to the Arrow, that where it lights it kils.

1810 *Sporting Mag.* XXXV. 300 They killed in one of the new plantations near Blankney.

1883 W. Black in *Harper's Mag.* Dec. 64/2 They had not been 'killing' at any of the farms.

e. *intr.* in passive sense: To be killed; to suffer killing. Of an animal: To yield (so much meat) when killed. Also, *to kill out*.

1857 *Jrnl. R. Agric. Soc.* XVIII. i. 162 On inquiry of butchers..I find that one characteristic of a beast which kills well, is to have a little stomach.

1888 *Whitby Gaz.* 25 Feb. 4/7, I saw the cow in the slaughter-house... She killed 34 stones.

1950 *N.Z. Jrnl. Agric.* Apr. 364/1 The Southdown has the advantage over the Leicester in that its progeny are quicker maturing and kill out at prime weight and at an earlier age (3 to 4 months).

1971 *Country Life* 30 Dec. 1857/3 Limousin-sired fat cattle killed out at 68 per cent; far above our national average for our native breeds.

f. *trans.* To procure (meat) by killing animals.

1560 Bible (Genev.) *1 Sam.* xxv. 11 My bread, & my water, & my flesh that I haue killed for my sherers.

1689 Luttrell *Brief Rel.* (1857) I. 511 The lords of the admiralty have sent orders..to kill beefe and pork for 65 men of war.

1838 James *Robber* vi, The beef was not killed at the end of the table.

"Jehovah" Versus "Yahweh"

QUESTION #568

I read the article, "*The Deity Named Yahweh*," from the web. Is it true that in the Hebrew alphabet there is no "J"? You say the proper name is "*Jehovah*." As for myself, I prefer Yahweh. I am not a biblical scholar but have read enough from those that are who prefer the use of Yahweh. Which is one reason I like the *Holman Christian Standard Bible*. It retains the name Yahweh throughout OT Scripture.

ANSWER #568

There is no "J," but the Hebrew "YODH" is transliterated as a "J" like in Greek the rough breathing "IOTA" is translated "J" like JESUS for IESOUS.

I believe that the word, "*Yahweh*," is a false term for the LORD which has many downsides. The vowel points underneath YHWH are clear that it should be written and pronounced as "*Jehovah*."

The *Holman Christian Standard Bible* is in error here as it is in many, many other places. You can see evidences of this in my booklet, *Holes In The Holman Standard Bible* (**BFT #2966 @ $6.00 + $4.00 S&H**).

Lucifer's Identity And Power

QUESTION #569

Dr. Kent Hovind claims that Lucifer fell from heaven during the creation mentioned in Genesis 1 and 2. What do you think?

ANSWER #569

The Bible doesn't tell us when Lucifer fell, only that he fell. Obviously he had the power to test Adam and Eve to disobey God. He still had access to God in the book of Job. He had the power to test the Lord Jesus Christ. At some point "*the accuser of the brethren*" (Revelation 12:10) will be cast out of heaven.

Zechariah And Jeremiah

QUESTION #570

Were Zechariah and Jeremiah contemporaries? Could Zechariah have written what he heard Jeremiah say?

ANSWER #570

Yes, that might have been possible. Jeremiah lived into the Babylonian captivity. Haggai, Zechariah, and Malachi prophesied after the exile, so they

were very close to being contemporary. Doubters will never be convinced.
You sometimes have to give up on them. Let the doubters doubt. After you
solve one problem, they often bring up 50 or 100 others.

The Tabernacle Past And Future
QUESTION #571

1. I have questions on the tabernacle mentioned in the Old Testament and
some future fulfillment. From the reading, the tabernacle seems to have been
a temporary shelter, a tent type of thing, that was portable. I have heard it
mentioned that there are some who think that the eventual rebuilt temple in
Jerusalem could be a tent, something quickly put together, rather than a
building. Do you think so?

2. In the O.T., was there actual worship done by people in the tent?
Were there musicians in there, people singing, in the Tabernacle of David?

3. The Tabernacle of David, mentioned in Amos 9:11, is that going to be
rebuilt during the Millennial Kingdom? Is that something different from a
Temple?

4. Also, I've heard people saying that prophesy is being fulfilled about
Isaiah 51:3, because Israel has irrigated the desert and there are many flowers
and fruit, an abundance of it, growing there now--that it is a shadow of things
coming. Can that possibly be a shadow of things or a beginning of fulfillment?
It doesn't seem like it could be because there is still the Tribulation Period,
which will be devastating on the earth--and seems like it couldn't happen until
the actual Millennial Kingdom.

ANSWER #571

1. <u>No. The millennial temple has dimensions that could not be tent-like</u>,
or it would be very difficult to make it fit.

2. <u>The people did not "_worship_" in the "_tent_._</u>" Only the priests were
allowed to enter. The people could only be outside the holy place in the court.

3. I think this could be taken literally rather than spiritually.

4. Though what they are doing is similar, <u>God will transform an entire
desert into a place where things can grow</u>. This literal fulfillment will take
place only by the Lord Himself during the millennial reign of Christ.

"Son Of A Year"
QUESTION #572

I was mainly concerned with the Hebrewist phrase "_son of a year_" which
Reina and Valera (and 1865) used to translate the first part of the verse. Allow
me to rephrase my question: Is being overly Hebrewist or literal here and in
other parts considered faulty?

ANSWER #572

I believe that the Hebrew expression, "*son of a year,*" usually means that the person is "*one year old.*" That would be the way we should usually translate this literal phrase, not "*son of a year.*"

Understanding Psalm 8:4-5

QUESTION #573

You state, on page 109 of *Defending the King James Bible*, that the new versions use "*dynamic equivalence*" in Psalm 8:4-5: "*Thou hast made him a little lower than the angels.*" Some new versions say "*a little lower than God.*"

Those who criticize the King James Bible with error here point out that the Hebrew is the plural name for "*God*" not "*angels.*" The word used for angel(s) in other places is #4397.

I can understand contextually by looking at the New Testament where the Greek is the word for "*angels.*" But what is the textual reason for changing the word used for "*God*" (gods) only in this place in the Old Testament to "*angels*"?

Doesn't that give room for the new versions to say the King James Bible is also using a form of "*dynamic equivalence*"?

According to my Bible Software program it says "*than the angels,*" is MEE-LOHIYM. Does the "MEE" stand for "*than the*"?

ANSWER #573

To illustrate that ELOHIM is not limited to "*God,*" but also "*judges,*" you can find many such uses (Exodus 21:6; 22:8; 22:9 (two places), and I stopped looking.

John 10:34-35 speaks of "*ye are gods*" (from Psalm 82:6 and Isaiah 41:23). This refers to ELOHIM as meaning "*judges.*"

"*Angel*" and "*angels*" in the Hebrew are not confined to MALAK, but Psalm 68:17 it is SHINAWN. Psalm 78:25 it is ABBEER, etc.

The Hebrew Lexicon meanings can be taken without calling any of the meanings as "*dynamic equivalency.*"

Here are some of the meanings of ELOHIM:

1) (plural)

  1a) **rulers, judges**

  1b) divine ones

  1c) **angels**

  1d) gods

2) (plural intensive - singular meaning)

2a) god, goddess

2b) <u>godlike one</u>

2c) works or special possessions of God

2d) the (true) God

2e) God

If "*angels*" in the plural is one correct translation of ELOHIM, why should this be called "*dynamic equivalency*"?

Genesis 6:2--Sons Of God
QUESTION #574

In Genesis 6:2, "*sons of God*" is a very obscure term. Can you give your interpretation? As for me, I believe it to mean fallen angels. What do you think?

ANSWER #574

I agree with you on the "*sons of God*" referring to fallen angels. The expression refers to angels in Job 1:6; 2:1, and 38:7.

Proverbs 26:4-5
QUESTION #575

I am liking my Defined KJV. The size is OK and the print is very good for my old cataract eyes. I like the fact that I do not have to run to Strong or otherwise to learn what a lot of words mean in today's language.

What would be your take on Proverbs 26:4-5?

ANSWER #575

These verses mean to me that we should put "*foolish*" people in their place. Depending on what folly they have done, they must be dealt with. God does not want His people to be foolish like the fools. The rebuke must be entirely based on the Words of God rather than the philosophy of the fools. It is a totally different method of argument when we use God's Words rather than man's worldly wisdom.

Isaiah 48:16 Explained
QUESTION #576

According to my Bible study program for Isaiah 48:16, the Hebrew says "*LORD God hath sent me and his Spirit.*"

The KJB text translates this: "*the Lord GOD, and his Spirit, hath sent me.*" Is the order in which the Hebrews read somehow indicated in the Hebrew words to explain the change in order of these words? The versions below have followed the order of the Hebrew words.

"And now the Lord GOD has sent Me, and His Spirit." NASV

"And now the Lord GOD and His Spirit have sent Me." NKJV

ANSWER #576

The order of Hebrew is as you have indicated it. <u>Often the Hebrew order of words is different from the English order. I believe the KJB is correct in interpreting "*and His Spirit*" as the compound subject of the verb "*sent*," rather than the object of that verb.</u> In ELOHIM ETH HASHAMAIM WA ETH HAARETZ. The order of the Hebrew is Hebrew, usually before a direct object the word ETH is used, like Genesis 1:1, BARA *"Created God"* [instead of *"God Created"*(Direct Object) *the heaven and* (Direct Object) *the earth."*

Absent the ETH (direct object indicator), <u>I would agree with the KJB and take "*and His Spirit*" as part of the compound subject rather than the direct object of the verb, send.</u>

Proverbs 18:24

QUESTION #577

I was recently challenged on the accuracy of the translation into English of the word *"friendly"* in Proverbs 18:24. I am stumped as to why that word is used. Can you provide some insight? Thank you.

ANSWER #577

I checked four Hebrew reference books and looked further into Proverbs 18:24. I found out that there are two readings for *"show himself friendly"* in Hebrew in this verse. In both readings the first two Hebrew letters are the same (reading from right to left, as Hebrew does), but the third letter was different. The one reading is *"friendly"* and the other reading is *"unfriendly or evil"* which is the exact opposite.

The KJB translators obviously took the *"friendly"* Hebrew reading for reasons known only to them and translated it accurately. .

To illustrate with English letters, it would be YYR (the Evil root reading) and HYR (the Friendly root reading).

It is interesting that the following use the *"friendly"* root:

1. New King James
2. Revised Webster's Bible
3. Regular Webster's Bible
4. Young's Literal Translation
5. Douay Rheims version
6. Modern Greek Bible

Daniel 3:25--The Son Of God

QUESTION #578

I have returned, since last year, to the King James Bible. Thank you for your websites. I know that everything you say about Bibliology, the Bible texts, and the doctrine of the preservation of the Words of God and the doctrine of inspiration is true. And, I agree with everything the DBS says about the modern perversions. We are in the end of this age of apostasy. There is no doubt in my mind.

In my telephone conversation with a person, we are discussing Dan. 3:25. I know the King James translators translated BAR ELAHH correctly as "*like the Son of God*." Good's perversion reads like most modern versions "*like a son of the gods*." He says ELAH is plural. He says in the LXX it is singular. I read Pastor Shonhaar's article and he mentions Dr. Thomas Strouse saying that BAR ELAHIN is a word pair. If the second word of a word pair is definite (God), then the first word is definite (the Son). I would appreciate any help you can give me in supporting the KJB's rendering of Dan 3:25.

It is really true: The King James Bible is a really different book. It is not the same book as the modern versions. It is the Holy Bible, the most precise English translation with all the words of God intact in it.

ANSWER #578

As far as Daniel 3:25 is concerned, the Aramaic word for God is apparently plural, but so is the Hebrew word for God, ELOHIM. The Hebrew is almost always properly translated as a Singular because God is a trinity with unity. He is a tri-unity. God is manifested in three Persons, but He is only one God. I would believe that the same is true of this Aramaic word for God. The king called these three Hebrew men "'*servants of the most high God*." (v. 26) yet this is the same word, yet it is translated singular here. Why not in v. 25?

Zechariah 5:9--Two Angels?

QUESTION #579

Could you folks shed some light on Zechariah 5:9 for us? Were these "*two women*" angels?

ANSWER #579

Zechariah 5:9 speaks of "*two women*" with "*wings like the wings of a stork.*" Without getting into the imagery here, let me answer the question of whether or not these two women were angels. I do not believe they were angels because, in verse 10, it talks about "*the angel that talked with me.*" This angel has nothing to do with the two women with wings. Therefore, I don't think the two women were angels.

Breaking Seven-Year Sabbaths

QUESTION #580

Was there a specific time from the Monarchy to the Captivity (490 years) that Israel broke the annual seven-year Sabbaths?

ANSWER #580

I think these quotes might be right as far as they go (monarchy to captivity and 490 years), but Daniel's 70 weeks of years (490 years) do not go from monarchy to captivity, but *"from the going forth of the commandment to restore and to build Jerusalem unto the Messiah the Prince."* (Daniel 9:25).

Was Samuel a Priest?

QUESTION #581

I had the question of whether Samuel was a priest in addition to a prophet (seer) and judge. Would appreciate your comments. The different Levitical administrations are sometimes confusing to me. I believe Samuel was of Levitical descent. I came up with these verses to consider.

Psalms 99:6 *"Moses and Aaron among **his priests, and Samuel among them** that call upon his name; they called upon the LORD, and he answered them."*

Jeremiah 15:1 *"Then said the LORD unto me, **Though Moses and Samuel stood before me**, yet my mind could not be toward this people: cast them out of my sight, and let them go forth."*

1 Samuel 2:18 *"But **Samuel ministered before the LORD**, being a child, girded with a linen ephod."*

ANSWER #581

I think the following verse shows Samuel to be a prophet:

1 Samuel 9:9 (*"Beforetime in Israel, when a man went to enquire of God, thus he spake, Come, and **let us go to the seer**: for **he that is now called a Prophet was beforetime called a Seer**."*)

Eli, the priest, trained Samuel to be a priest also.

1 Samuel 13:12 *"Therefore said I, The Philistines will come down now upon me to Gilgal, and I have not made supplication unto the LORD: **I forced myself therefore, and offered a burnt offering**."*

1 Samuel 13:13 *"And **Samuel said to Saul, Thou hast done foolishly**: thou hast not kept the commandment of the LORD thy God, which he commanded thee: for now would the LORD have established thy kingdom upon Israel for ever."*

This shows that Samuel was to make the offering as a priest, not Saul who was only a king.

CHAPTER VIII
QUESTIONS ABOUT
MISCELLANEOUS
SUBJECTS

1. VARIOUS BOOKS

Date Of Strong's "Old Edition"
QUESTION #582
Which year did the "old edition" of *Strong's Exhaustive Concordance* come out, if you know? Is the "old edition" different from the newer ones?
ANSWER #582
Try around 1940 through 1960 for the date and ask if they have the ERV (1881) or RV as it may be called in the APPENDIX when it differs from the KJB. The ASV of 1901 and the RSV of 1881 are virtually identical in both the OT and NT. I recommend you get an "old edition" of *Strong's Exhaustive Concordance* where he has made note of the differences between the KJB and the RSV.

Interpretarion of Genesis 6:1-4
QUESTION #583
Do you have a complete study on Genesis ? What is your belief and interpretation on Gen. 6:1-4 ?
ANSWER #583
We have the following on Genesis:
BFT #2555   177pp. $18.00   Gems from Genesis--Comments and Questions by Waite, Dr. D. A.
BFT #2824/1-7   Cassettes $21.00   Genesis 1-3--Exposition and

Applications for Today   by Waite, Dr. D. A.

BFT #2824VCI-2   VCR $25.00   Genesis 1-3--Exposition and Applications for Today   by Waite, Dr. D. A

BFT #2824   103pp. $10.00   Genesis 1-3--Matthew Henry's Comments + KJB & Hebrew   by Waite, Dr. D. A.

BFT #2523/1-7   Cassettes $21.00   Genesis Expounded Verse by Verse--Bible Institute Class (Phila.)   by Waite, Dr. D. A.

BFT #2523VC1-2   VCR $25.00   Genesis Expounded Verse by Verse--Bible Institute Class (Phila.)   by Waite, Dr. D. A.

BFT #2563/1-4   Cassettes $12.00   Genesis Expounded--Gems From Genesis   by Waite, Dr. D. A.

BFT #2563VCR   VCR $15.00   Genesis Expounded--Gems From Genesis   by Waite, Dr. D. A.

BFT #0445   716pp. $28.00   Genesis Record, The   by Morris, Dr. Henry

BFT #1522/1-5   Cassettes $15.00   Genesis--A Survey Of The Book by Waite, Dr. D. A.

I believe that Genesis 6:1-4 speaks of the cohabitation of "*the sons of God*" with the daughters of men. I believe that the "*sons of God*" are clearly identified in Job as being fallen angels (Job 1:6; 2:1; 38:7).

Strong's Concordance

QUESTION #584

Is there a 1611 KJV on computer program out there, where I can read the 1611 KJV on my computer screen? How about a computerized *Strong's Concordance*? Which one do you use?

ANSWER #584

I use and recommend the Logos Bible Software for the Hebrew, Aramaic, Greek, the King James Bible, and many of the other versions.

This system has a *Strong's Concordance* in it as well. You can locate it on Google. Just type in Logos Bible Software, and you can find it.

Various Good Textbooks

QUESTION #585

I wanted your recommendation on good textbooks to use for our hermeneutics and Old Testament Survey classes this fall. I was also wondering about some good Greek material on perhaps DVD or video. I already have *Beginners Grammar Of The Greek New Testament* by William Hersey Davis, so it would be nice to have something that corresponds with that. Any help you could give me on organizing a small Bible Institute schedule would be appreciated.

ANSWER #585

Rollin Chafer has a good book on hermeneutics which is out of print. I have a copy machine copy of it which I could copy for you.

I don't know about O.T. survey.

I have an introductory video on beginning Greek, and also a course on First Year Greek and Second Year Greek with use of *Davis' Beginner's Greek Grammar* used and that of Dana and Mantey for *Intermediate Grammar.*

Hebrew Reference Books

QUESTION #586

Hebrew reference books. Could you please explain to me how the Hebrew reference books you prefer relate to the Masoretic Text?

ANSWER 586

The *Analytical Hebrew Lexicon* that I recommend to everyone shows the specific forms of the Hebrew Words as used in the Old Testament and the Hebrew root form. You can then go to that root form for the various meanings of the Word.

Moorman's Majority Text Book

QUESTION #587

I forgot to ask about Dr. Jack Moorman's *MajorityText* book whether this covers the subject adequtely?

ANSWER #587

Dr. Moorman's book is the best coverage against the *Majority Text* in print. It is **BFT #1617 @ $20.00 + $7.00 S&H.** You need no other book on this. As of now, Dr. H. D. Williams has put this excellent book into a Print On Demand (POD) book. I hope it gets wide distribution. Before this POD book, it has been only in copy machine format.

Value Of Strong's Concordance

QUESTION #588

What's your take on looking up Greek words using Strong's dictionary or other dictionaries? Should I direct people to your products? If so can I get a website address for them so I can point them directly to these products?

ANSWER #588

Though *Strong's Exhaustive Concordance* is a helpful tool for English-speaking Christians, the best Greek Lexicon for those looking for Greek definitions, in my opinion, is the *New Analytical Greek Lexicon* by Pershbacher. It is about $35.00. With cash or credit card up front, we can special order it and have it drop shipped from the publisher to the person who orders it. It gives every Greek form as it occurs in the Greek N.T. and then gives the root so people can look up the meaning of the root.

Like in English, if you have the word "went," no one, unfamiliar with English, would have any idea that this word was the past tense of the verb "go." By analogy, this Greek Analytical Lexicon would tell them, when they looked up the word as it appeared in the New Testament, where the root word was. They could then go to that root word and find out all of its meanings. People can go to either BibleForToday.org or DeanBurgonSociety.org and search these sites for many books dealing with subjects taught in the Bible.

Hebrew & Greek Grammar Books
QUESTION #589

I am a born-again believer. I have enjoyed reviewing your site along with the Way of Life site. Many years ago I studied Hebrew & Greek via Correspondence through Southeastern Bible College & Moody Bible Institute. Unfortunately I did not keep up with it and lost most of my skills. Can you recommend a reliable Hebrew & Greek grammar for me to get up to speed again?

ANSWER #589

For an intermediate grammar in Greek, I recommend Dana and Mantey's *Manual Grammar of the Greek New Testament*. It may be out of print, but it is still available at present on Amazon.com.

I recommend a beginning Hebrew Grammar which also might be out of print but is available from Amazon.com. It is *Introduction to Biblical Hebrew* by Thomas O. Lambdin. These books can be used to go along with my 2nd year Greek and 1st year Hebrew courses which are available. Here is how you can get my first and second year Greek courses:

> **BFT #1260/1-37** Cassettes **$150.00** N.T.Greek Course-8 Sem.Hrs. (40-2hr. cassettes.; +Grammar) (B) Waite, Dr. D. A.
>
> **BFT #1064/1-30** Cassettes **$80.00** Second Year Greek--Translation of John & Exegesis--30 cassettes. Waite, Dr. D. A. (Dana & Mantey textbook is extra)
>
> My first year Greek course, including the textbook can be viewed without charge at http://www.biblefortoday.org/greek.htm if you wish to do so. My

first year Hebrew course can be obtained as:

BFT #1162/1-40 Cassettes **$175.00** Biblical Hebrew Course (40 Cassettes; 80 Hours) Waite, Dr. D. A.

Don't Order These Numbers
QUESTION #590

Would I be correct in presuming that booklet # 0470 includes the points covered by tract # 0238; seeing as the former is 85 pages & latter only 16, yet cover the same subject?

ANSWER #590

I wouldn't order either of these.   When these booklets were written, "*Majority Text*" was a term that meant the Textus Receptus. But now, after 1980 or so, it means either the Hodges/Farstad Greek Text or the Robinson/Pierpoint Greek Text. I write against both of these current so-called "Majority" Texts. If you want a defense of the TR, I would suggest you begin with my book, *Defending the King James Bible* (**BFT #1594** @ **$12.00 + $7.00 S&H**.)

If you want a critique against the so-called "MAJORITY" Text of Hodges and Farstad, you should get **BFT #1617   160 pp. $20.00 + $7.00 S&H** *Hodges/Farstad 'Majority' Text Refuted By Evidence* By Moorman, Dr. Jack

A Good Hebrew Grammar
QUESTION #591

Thank you for your email and Greek Grammar recommendation. When you get a chance, please drop me an email with the Hebrew Grammar title you mentioned.

ANSWER #591

The book is *Introduction to Biblical Hebrew* by Thomas O. Lambdin. He is from Harvard University and certainly not a Fundamentalist, but this text was recommended by one of my classmates from Dallas Seminary (1948-1952). Dr. D. Duane Young, who is a Bible-believing Hebrew scholar, thought this book was the best for us to use, so we used it.

2. Bible For Today Materials

How To Get On Our Website
QUESTION #592
How can a person get on your website and (1) listen to your audio and video programs and (2) find how to get your books and materials?

ANSWER #592
HOW TO LISTEN TO BOTH LIVE & DELAYED MEETINGS

From the Bible For Today Baptist Church

900 Park Avenue, Collingswood, NJ 08108

With Pastor D. A. Waite, Th.D., Ph.D.

Phone: 856-854-4747;

E-mail: BFT @BibleForToday.org

Website: www.BibleForToday.org

If you have a **high speed computer**, you can **SEE and HEAR** our services by Internet in your own home 24-hours a day, 7 days a week, 365 days each year. If you have a **dial-up computer**, you can **HEAR** these services & maybe **SEE** a little. Here's what you can do:

I. **FOR LISTENING TO CURRENT SERVICES LIVE**:
   A. Go to www.BibleForToday.org, and click on the **BROWN BOX** at the following times:
   1. Sundays at 10 a.m. (Eastern)
Verse by verse preaching in one of the books of the New Testament
   2. Sundays at 1:30 p.m. (Eastern)
Verse by verse Bible teaching discussion in one of the books of the New Testament.
   3. Thursdays at 8:00 p.m. (Eastern) Verse by verse Bible teaching discussion in an Old Testament Book.

II. **FOR LISTENING TO CURRENT SERVICES BY DELAY**:
If you miss these LIVE messages, you can see them 24/7 the following seven days as follows:
   A. Go to www.BibleForToday.org and click on the **YELLOW BOX** where there are many messages on this **YELLOW BOX**, one after the other:
   1. The 1st program is our 10 a.m.verse-by-verse preaching from one of the books of the New

Testament

2. The 2nd program is our 1:30 p.m. Bible teaching discussion from one of the books of the New Testament

3. The 3rd program is our last Thursday's Bible teaching discussion in one of the books of the Old Testament

4. The 4th program is Dr. H. D. Williams' Upper Room Bible Study from Cleveland, GA (heard Tuesdays at 7 p.m. Eastern)

5. The 5th program is Daniel Waite's weekly Theology Class from Dr. Lewis Sperry Chafer's *Systematic Theology* text.

6. The 6th program is Daniel Waite's tutorial with Jack Silverstein on various Bible books.

7. The 7th program is Daniel Waite's 1st year Greek class

III. For **EARLIER RECORDED SERVICES FROM ROMANS THROUGH REVELATION** on a 16-week cycle

A. Go to www.BibleForToday.org

1. Click on the **BROWN BOX**.

a. You can listen to Earlier Recorded Services 24 hours a day, 7 days a week, 365 days per year.

b. Each service is a verse-by-verse Bible preaching and teaching from a New Testament book.

2. These messages go from Romans through Revelation.

3. It takes 16 weeks to go through all of these 22 New Testament Books.

Why I Don't Answer Some E-Mails

QUESTION #593

Why you did not answer any of my questions that I asked you in the past? It confuses me. You are well taught and yet you won't answer any of my Biblical questions I asked you.

ANSWER #593

The reason, as I told you, that I did not answer you on E-mails is that I did not want to get into an endless discussion of things that you and I differ on. The best way to discuss things is in person or on the phone, rather than with endless E-mails. There are some things that we must just agree to disagree and go on being friends. I would be glad to discuss all of these matters if you phone me at 856-854-4747.

How to Pay On-Line
QUESTION #594

I am writing on behalf on Nikola Vukov, from Croatia, Europe. I am an independent Baptist missionary working with Nikola and one other man on translating the Bible into the Croatian language. Brother Nikola saw your Bible on-line and ordered it to help him in the translation work that he is doing. I believe he needs to pay you in two installments. He asked if I would pay it, and he would pay me back. Can I pay on-line? Please advise the best payment method.

ANSWER #594

Yes, you can pay online. Just go to BibleForToday.org and click on the BFT WEBSTORE. Or, you can pay by credit card. I hope your Croatian translation is faithful to the Textus Receptus.

---

3. Local Church Matters

Importance Of Sound Church Music
QUESTION #595

I have a question. I am Afrikaans (Dutch) so I am familiar with a confession of faith in my mother tongue and I am not so familiar with it in English. I use The Baptist Confession of Faith (1689). With slight revisions by C. H. Spurgeon. Would you say it is correct for me to quote it and use it? I also only use KJV Bible but my real question is: I am now fellowshipping with a church that allows modern music. On two occasions now---two different pastors preached. The one's doctrine on salvation was incorrect (he said we are not once saved always saved, but can lose it). The other said a church should be run like a business. They also have the prosperity mentality. I then looked at their statement of faith on the web page and I find it troublesome. Would you mind having a look and let me know if you agree. If so, then, should I completely sever my ties with them because I have been having a hard time in the church?

They also "attacked" me by saying I create conflict because of my stance on doctrine and church music. There is no other church I can attend. They are all the same (modern & dead). My spirit feels very heavy. I feel that the one person is used to derail me. Instead of praising God I end up being critical. Oh and another thing, they gossip and lie. Should I take this as an indication that they are not spiritually alive or just immature? I wish to honour my Lord and Saviour and I don't want to take heed of what men think.

I am looking forward to your service on Sunday morning and hope to watch (DV). I don't have a copy of your hymnal so I wonder if you have one of the following hymns? The Lord is our Shepherd Psalm 23 Holy, holy, holy.

ANSWER #595

I am very glad you received my E-mail about our church services on the BROWN BOX and the YELLOW BOX and that you are able to view them in that way.

Regarding Spurgeon's Baptist (London) Confession of faith, I think it is all right on the whole. I would disagree with the provisions which limit the death of our Saviour only to the "*elect*." I believe He died for the sins of the whole world, but only those who genuinely receive and trust him are saved. I believe in Biblical dispensations rather than in so-called "*covenant theology*." I also believe in Daniel's 70th week or the seven-year tribulation preceded by the rapture of all saved people and followed by the 1,000 year reign on this earth of the Lord Jesus Christ. So these are some of things in this Confession that I would differ with, the 32 articles of this confession. Many of the articles are sound and Biblical. You can compare that Confession with our Articles of Faith at http://biblefortoday.org/bft_articles_faith.htm if you wish to look them over.

As to your situation in your local church there, the Lord must lead you about it. You are right that once we are saved, we cannot be lost. You are also correct in your stand on good sound church music. If they are attacking you, perhaps it is time to "*sever your ties*" with them, as you put it. I don't know your stand on fellowship by way of the Internet with our 𝕭𝕚𝕭𝕝𝕖 𝔣𝕠𝕣 𝕿𝕠𝕕𝕒𝕪 𝕭𝕒𝕡𝕥𝕚𝕤𝕥 𝕮𝕙𝕦𝕣𝕔𝕙, but we would welcome you to attend in that way regularly if you so chose to do so.

We could send you a copy of our Hymnal. We could also send you each month a DVD with the four weeks of previous services for your listening at any time of the day or night. I know even in this country it is difficult to find a good sound church with expository verse-by-verse preaching, using the King James Bible, and with traditional music such as ours. How much more difficult there in your foreign country. Please let me know your answers to the Hymnal and/or DVD's and we'll be happy to do whatever you wish. We'll be praying for you, that our Lord might lead you into His most blessed will for your life at this time.

Baptism And The Lord's Supper
QUESTION #596

What is the biblical explanation about children of all ages who are not baptized but eat the Lord's Supper? The elders or deacons give them it or at times the pastor does same.

ANSWER #596

I realize that historic Baptist doctrine is that only Scripturally baptized people should partake of the Lord's Supper. I believe this would refer to their being obedient to the N.T. which states that we should be "*baptizing them in the Name of the Father, and of the Son, and of the Holy Ghost*" (Matthew 28:19). Without being baptized, there is a perception of being disobedient and therefore not living up to the following verses:

1 Corinthians 11:28-29: "*But let a man examine himself, and so let him eat of that bread, and drink of that cup. For he that eateth and drinketh unworthily, eateth and drinketh damnation to himself, not discerning the Lord's body.*"

Though I realize this position and respect it, and all of our children have been baptized, I stress that people must be saved and born-again and walking with the Lord before partaking. I believe each local church must make their own decision on this and I will respect their decisions.

4. Old Testament Hebrew

The Hebrew Letters SIN and SHIN
QUESTION #597
In the Bible program I have for Hebrew where they show the alphabet, they have a dot above both "SIN" and "SHIN" but in different places at the top of the letter. Is that an error? They also have a dot in the middle of "BETH" which is omitted in Psalm 119 in my Bible (the dot, that is.) And the dot above "SHIN" in my KJ Bible is not there.

ANSWER #597
On the SIN and SHIN, if the dot is on the left, it is a SIN. If the dot is on the right, it is SHIN. In some of the King James Bibles, if the Hebrew letters are used, you can see the proper use of the dots. You can see the names of these letters in Psalm 119:161-168 in Hebrew at the beginning of each verse. The following verses have the SIN (Dot left): v. 161, 162, 166. The other five verses in the section of the SHIN (Dot right).

Biblical Hebrew Class
QUESTION #598
The reason I am writing is to ask if you still have a class on Biblical Hebrew? I would also like to ask which copy of the Hebrew text should I get for my personal study? I do not know which one is included in the TR.

ANSWER #598
I think the Hebrew text that is closest to that underlying the KJB Hebrew is the Letteris Text printed by the British and Foreign Bible Society. It comes in a parallel KJB and Hebrew. We carry it. I think it is now up to $70.00 each.

Since you are searching for information on this KJB/TR situation, if you would like to receive it, and if you would send me your address, I would be glad to send you, with my compliments, my book, *Defending the King James Bible--A Fourfold Superiority*. In the Appendix, I have listed over 1,000 other titles defending the KJB and its underlying Hebrew, Aramaic, and Greek Words. This might help you see what is out there at least.

I don't have a present Hebrew class, but I have a series of classes on MP-3 and audio cassettes on an 8-semester class on first year Hebrew which are available.

If you are interested in some of my Preaching Verse By Verse books, they are available. These are from my own sermons. I have the following available:

(1) 1 Peter, (2) Romans, (3) Galatians, (4) Ephesians, (5) Philippians, (6) Colossians and Philemon, (7) 1 Timothy, and (8) 2 Timothy. In the old Dallas Theological Seminary, Dr. Chafer, the Founder and my teacher for four years, taught us to be expository (verse by verse) preachers and teachers of the Words of God. That is what I have sought to do in each service of our church. The motto of my seminary then (and I guess now) was *"Preach the Word"* (KERUXON TON LOGON).

The Hebrew Old Testament
QUESTION #599

No, I don't have *Defending the King James Bible* yet. I should pick up a copy of your book! Does chapter 2 go into detail with differences in wording in the Kittel and the Ben Chayyim texts? I am looking for a listing of all the "major" differences in the Old Testament. Most scholars spend the time defending the Greek underlying the KJV. I know both the Hebrew and the Greek underlying the KJV are far superior. I am just looking for a listing and comparison of words. Does chapter 2 go into this in depth? A friend of mine thought you may have compiled a document I could buy that has these differences enumerated.

ANSWER #599

I don't know of anyone who has made up a list of differences between the Ben Chayyim Hebrew text and the Ben Asher text. I have been seeking for these quantitative differences for many years, but no one has been willing to come up with this tedious research. It would involve the scanning of the Ben Chayyim Hebrew text and then compare it to the already scanned Ben Asher text.

The Trinitarian Bible Society (TBS) of the UK thinks there are only about 8 changes, but if this be so, why did Rudolf Kittel's 1906 and 1912 follow Ben Chayyim and his 1937 change from the Ben Chayyim and begin to follow the Ben Asher? There are bound to be many differences. Sorry for my lack of information. My Chapter 2 just lays out that there are different Hebrew and Greek texts and explains what they are.

5. Prophecy

The Judgment Of The Nations
QUESTION #600
I recently heard a sermon where the preacher said that Matthew 25:30 ("*And cast ye the unprofitable servant into outer darkness: there shall be weeping and gnashing of teeth*") refers to carnal believers at the Judgment Seat of Christ. Not that they will be eternally condemned, but that it described those who would suffer loss "*yet so as by fire.*" Is this how you understand that passage?

ANSWER #600
Matthew 25:31-46 is the judgment of the nations. It is after the Lord's return to the earth in glory. The goat nations on His left will be sent to everlasting hell fire (v. 41 and 46).

The parable of the talents (coming just before this judgment of the nations (Matthew 25:14-30). Verse 30 might also be the fate in hell fire of those who pretended to be true followers of the Saviour, but who were professing only without possessing. Matthew 7:20-23 speaks also of such that profess but do not possess. This is as I see it at present. I do not believe Matthew 25 in any of its verses refers to the Judgment Seat of Christ for saved people, whether carnal or spiritual.

The Two Witnesses In Revelation
QUESTION #601
Who do you think the two witnesses in Revelation will be?

ANSWER #601
I think the two witnesses are identified by the miracles they will perform. One set of miracles are similar to those performed by Moses. The other set of miracles are similar to those performed by Elijah. For this reason, I believe the two witnesses will be Moses and Elijah.

6. Divorce And Remarriage

Divorced And Remarried Pastors?

QUESTION #602

A quick question for you with regard to the ministry. It is my understanding that the Bible would seem to teach that a man who has had more than one wife cannot be in the ministry. This question is important to me because you see I have been widowed and got remarried. Since then, my wife has divorced me. I wanted nothing to do with the divorce. I am still standing for my marriage. I do have an interest in doing something for the Lord. I want to know if I qualify. I would really appreciate your comments.

ANSWER #602

Your second marriage was Scriptural, but your divorce (though not desired by you) puts up a caution because of some of the qualifications in 1 Timothy 3:2-7 "*blameless*" is a caution. "*Ruling well his own house*" is a second caution. A "*good report to them which are without*" is a third caution. Those who are lost might not agree that a divorced and remarried pastor has a "*good report*" as far as they are concerned. Titus 1:6 has "*blameless*" also. It would not be a good example of a Christian life. There are other ministries you could do without being a pastor. You should ask your local church which ministries they would be comfortable for them for you to be used for the Lord.

7. The Spanish Bible

Reina/Valera/Gomez Spanish Bible
QUESTION #603

Some people, like Calvin George, criticize us who use the Spanish Reina-Valera-Gomez (RVG) by saying that the Spanish 1960 edition was indeed a TR-based Bible. Would it be best for Dr Gomez and others of us to say that the RVG is base on the Traditional Text rather than the Textus Receptus? How much difference is there between the two?

ANSWER #603

I like to say I am following the Traditional Textus Receptus that underlies the King James Bible. This pins it down to those Words which are 99% the Words of Beza's 5th edition of 1598. There are only about 190 places where the KJB followed something other than Beza.

This is the text used in *Scrivener's Annotated New Testament* and the exact one used in the TBS Scrivener's text. This pins it down so everyone knows what we're referring to.

Dean Burgon used *"Received Text"* as a synomym for the *"Traditional Text."* I think we should use the Textus Receptus (TR) and specify it as the Words underlying the KJB. This nails it down firmly. This is the text Dr. Humberto Gomez used in his Spanish Reina-Valera-Gomez (RVG) and the one the KJB translators used.

8. The Dean Burgon Society

What Was Dean Burgon's Beliefs?

QUESTION #604

I have been given the impression that Burgon was, like Bishops Wordsworth and Wilberforce, Old High Church, as opposed to AngloCatholic. What is the truth? As Dean Burgon Society president, you ought to have an authoritative answer to questions on Dean Burgon.

ANSWER #604

Dean Burgon's specific theology was his own. Our Dean Burgon Society (DBS) does not hold to all of his theological position. We have our own theological position as listed in our *Articles of Faith*. You can see them here:
http://www.deanburgonsociety.org/DBS_Society/articles.htm

We used Dean Burgon's name for four major reasons: (1) because of his defense of the King James Bible; (2) because of his defense of the Traditional Hebrew, Aramaic, and Greek Words that underlie the KJB; (3) because of his sound and detailed exposure of the false Gnostic Critical Greek Westcott and Hort Greek text of his day; and (4) because of his sound and detailed exposure of the theory behind that text.

Index Of Words And Phrases

"inerrant" or "infallible" 47
"Jehovah" Versus "Yahweh" 138
(## 401-600) iii
$625,000 109
$625,000 to the apostate group 109
1 Corinthians 12:4-11 .... 45, 49
1 John 5:7-8 15
1 John 5:7-8 Problems 15
1% CT Greek MSS 16
1598 .... 4, 7, 8, 10, 11, 15, 18, 23, 34, 35, 40, 44, 57, 58, 103,
                                                128, 130, 165
1611 .... 23, 34, 39, 47, 48, 59, 64, 77, 78, 80, 93, 112, 115, 124,
                                                130, 132, 146
1611 KJV 132, 146
1881 .... 5, 10, 13, 24, 34, 92, 145
2 Chronicles 33:19 48
2 Thessalonians 2:2 68
2 Timothy 3:15-16 10
2,000, 4,000, 6,653+ 6
201-400 iii
356 doctrinal passages 5, 20, 32, 92, 93, 107, 116
356 passages 105
37 Historical Links 19
5,500 Greek N.T. manuscripts 6
5th edition of Beza 23
8,000 differences 5, 12, 18, 24, 28, 32, 33, 92, 107, 116
8,000 Differences Between The Critical Greek Text 5, 18, 28,
                                                          33
8,000 Differences Between the Critical Text 12
86,000 quotations 9
900 Park Avenue .... i, 151
99% TR 16
A Critical Answer To Michael Sproul's God's Word Preserved
         43
A Good Hebrew Grammar 149
A KJB Reformed Seminary 122
A man convinced against his will 12, 14, 15, 58
About the Author iv
Accurate Copies 10, 11, 46, 47

Acknowledgments . . . . ii, iv
Acts 12 70
additions, subtractions or other changes 6
Adoption 54, 55
adultery 42, 79, 94, 95, 101, 102
Advisory Council 27
agree to disagree 152
Alexandria 5, 9, 14, 18, 20, 24, 32, 33, 131
American Standard Version 104, 105
ANALYTICAL GREEK LEXICON 148
ANALYTICAL HEBREW LEXICON 147
Annotated Greek New Testament 10, 11, 19, 92, 130
Apocrypha 39, 47, 130
Aramaic 6, 11, 12, 30, 31, 38, 39, 43, 44, 47, 50, 54, 57, 64,
                  65, 75, 92, 104, 107, 109, 118, 120, 124-126, 129, 132,
                                          143, 146, 159, 167
articles 11, 53, 116, 117, 156, 167
ASV of 1901 145
baptism 132, 156
Baptism And The Lord's Supper 156
Baptist churches 37
Barbara Egan ii
Bart Ehrman 15
Bart Ehrman's False Views 15
BATTLEGROUND 13
Berry 10, 27
Beza 4, 7, 8, 10, 11, 15, 18, 23, 34, 35, 40, 44, 57, 58, 103,
                                          128, 130, 165
Beza's 5th edition 4, 8, 10, 11, 15, 18, 34, 35, 40, 44, 58, 103,
                                          128, 130, 165
BFT #1064/1-30 . . . . 27, 29, 148
BFT #1162/1-40 . . . . 27, 149
BFT #1260/1-37 . . . . 27, 148
BFT #1428 . . . . 6, 16, 18, 33, 34, 131, 132
BFT #1428 @ $20.00+ $7.00 S&H 18
BFT #1442 109
BFT #1594 . . . . 31, 47, 57, 65, 93, 118, 131, 149
BFT #1617 . . . . 10, 33, 147, 149
BFT #1643 @ $46.00 + $12.00 S&H 7
BFT #1670 . . . . 11, 17, 28, 35, 92, 130
BFT #186 10
BFT #186 @ $30.00 + $7.00 S&H 10

BFT #3032 9
BFT #3032 @ $20.00 + $7.00 S&H 9
BFT #3084 . . . . 5, 12, 18, 28, 32, 92
BFT #3138 . . . . 6, 13, 28, 92
BFT #3138 @ $25.00 + $7.00 S&H 6, 13
BFT #3230 . . . . 5, 92
BFT #3309 iii
BFT #3309 @ $12.00 + $7.00 S&H iii
BFT #3373 iii
BFT #3373 @ $12.00 + $7.00 S&H iii
BFT #3473 1
BFT #3482 1
BFT #3482 @ $12.00 + $7.00 S&P 1
BFT Phone: 856-854-4452 i
Bible College 44, 148
Bible For Today . . . . i-iv, 16, 29, 121, 151, 156
Bible For Today Baptist Church . . . . i-iii, 151, 156
Bible For Today materials . . . . iii, iv
Bible For Today Press i
Bible Preservation 39, 43, 57, 64
Bible Versions Controversy Basics 103
Biblical Creation In Genesis 1 53
Biblical Hebrew Class 159
Biblical Mathematics 54
bishop 5, 26, 41
bishops 167
BJU 43, 108, 115
black 9, 20, 121, 137
blood 15, 16, 52, 56, 58, 63, 98, 134
Bob Jones University 11, 43, 44, 108, 115
Body . . . . ii, 41, 42, 45, 49, 51, 55, 56, 72, 73, 80, 85, 98, 99, 101,
156
Bowe 125
British and Foreign Bible Society 159
British Museum 9, 25
BROWN BOX 63, 151, 152, 155
Bruce Metzger 15
Burgon . . . . ii-iv, 9, 10, 13-16, 18, 21, 25, 27, 32, 34, 40, 46, 125,
165, 167
buried in a Protestant cemetery 4

Byzantine 9, 11, 22, 33, 43, 130, 131
Calvary Baptist Seminary 43, 44
Calvinism 59, 122
Cambridge 13, 14, 47, 48, 119, 120, 123, 124, 127
Cambridge 1769 Text 119, 123, 127
Cambridge KJB 14, 47, 48
Cardinal Ximenes 7
Cardinal's hat 4
Catholic church 3, 4, 38, 39, 69
Catholic monastery 3, 4
Catholics 3, 4, 38, 39
Central Baptist Seminary 43, 44
Chafer 38, 147, 160
Chinese Union Version .... iii, iv, 68, 85-87, 89-101
Christmas 92
church .... i-iv, 3-5, 9, 14, 19-22, 25, 37-40, 45, 48-50, 61, 64, 68,
        69, 77, 92, 108, 119, 120, 126, 128, 131, 151, 155-157,
                                                160, 163, 167
Church Fathers 5, 9, 25, 40, 92, 131
Church Music 155, 156
Church Phone: 856-854-4747 i
Cloud 15
Codex B and Its Allies 7
Collingswood .... i, 151
Collingswood, New Jersey i
Collingswood, New Jersey 08108 i
Colophons 13, 14
Comfort 163
Complutensian Polyglot 7, 8, 11, 23, 44, 128
Copyright, 2010 i
Council at Nicea 39
Critical Text 3-5, 7-9, 11-13, 15, 16, 18, 29, 31, 33, 43, 100,
                                                        131
Cursives 16, 17
CUV 68, 85-87, 89-101
D. A. Waite .... 1, i, iii, 1, 13, 16, 19, 27, 28, 47, 92, 151
D. A. Waite, Jr. 13, 19, 28, 92
Dallas Theological Seminary 28, 29, 34, 38, 116, 160
Dana and Mantey 147
Daniel 3:25--The Son Of God 143
Daniel S. Waite ii
Dave Hunt 51, 52

Dave Hunt Denies Literal Hell Fire 51
David Otis Fuller 9
deacons 20, 156
Dead Sea Scrolls 44
Dean Burgon .... ii-iv, 9, 10, 13-16, 21, 27, 32, 34, 40, 46, 165,
                                                                      167
Dean Burgon Society .... ii-iv, 10, 15, 16, 34, 40, 46, 167
Dean John W. Burgon 125
Defending the King James Bible 11, 13, 20, 31, 38, 47, 57, 59,
                  65, 93, 103, 104, 118, 119, 131-133, 140, 149, 159, 160
Defined King James Bible .... iv, 14, 67, 107, 108, 110, 119-121,
                                                   123, 124, 127, 129
Defined King James Bible Order Form iv
Definitive KJB Video? 126
Demon-Possession 48
departure 52, 53, 68
Detroit Baptist Seminary 43, 44
Discrepancies In The KJB 125
Dispensationalism 42, 62
dispensations 42, 155
divorce .... iii, iv, 95, 120, 163
divorce and remarriage .... iii, iv, 163
Divorced And Remarried Pastors? 163
Doctored New Testament 6, 13, 19, 28, 92
Dr. and Mrs. H. D. Williams ii
Dr. Chafer 38, 160
Dr. Chester Kulas 125
Dr. D. A. Waite 1, 1, 16, 27
Dr. David Otis Fuller 9
Dr. Edward Hills 40
Dr. Floyd Nolan Jones 125
Dr. Frederick Scrivener 8, 11, 18
Dr. Gerardus Bowe 125
Dr. Gomez's Spanish Bible 14
Dr. Humberto Gomez 12, 165
Dr. Jack Moorman 6, 9, 25, 27, 34, 92, 131
Dr. Moorman 9, 16, 17
Dr. Thomas Strouse 143
Dr. Waite 16
Early Manuscripts, Church Fathers 5, 92

Early MSS, Church Fathers, and the Authorized Version 9
Easter 70, 71
Ecumenical Movement 37
Egan . . . . ii, 12, 14, 90, 93, 105
Ehrman 15
eight miscellaneous topics iii
Elect 33, 59, 63, 155
election 62
Elias 123, 127
Elzevir 7, 8, 23, 44, 70, 128
English Revised Version 6, 34, 92
Englishman's Greek New Testament 19
Ephesians 4:8-12 . . . . 45, 49
Erasmus 3, 4, 7, 8, 11, 14, 23, 44, 57, 128, 131
Erasmus in 1516 14
Erasmus's text of 1516 4
errors 7, 43, 47, 52, 92, 93, 105, 125, 130
ERV 4, 6, 34, 100, 145
ERV, NIV, NASV, ESV, RSV, NRSV, NEV 4
Esaias 123, 127
ESV 4, 6, 29, 100, 104, 108, 109, 115-117
ETH 142, 159
e-mail: BFT@BibleForToday.org i
Failures Of The NIV 110
Fallen Angels In Genesis 6? 64
False Bible Preservation 43
false doctrines 32
FALSE TEXT 18
fax: 856-854-2464 i
figure of speech 52
First Year Biblical Hebrew Course 27
Forever Settled 6, 16, 18, 33, 34, 131, 132
FOREWORD . . . . iii, iv
fornication 42, 79, 80, 94, 95
Free Course In 1st Year Greek 28
Fuller 9, 34
Gail Riplinger 65, 132
Galatians 5:19-21 42
Genesis 1:1 . . . . 54, 142
Geneva Bible 23, 103
George Ricker Berry 10, 27
Ghost 58, 59, 114, 156

Gnostic 5-9, 11, 13, 15-20, 24, 25, 28, 29, 31-34, 38, 52, 68,
               70, 92, 100, 104, 107, 109, 116, 129, 131, 132, 167
Gnostic Critical Greek Text 5, 6, 9, 19, 28, 32, 34, 38, 52, 68,
               70, 107, 109, 129, 131, 132
Gnosticism 5, 15
God Forbid 123, 124
God has preserved His Words 64
God the Holy Spirit 16, 48, 61, 90
God-breathed 10, 11
Gomez 12, 14, 165
Good Study Bibles 110
Gordon 9
Gospel of John 29
grammar 17, 29, 70, 77, 120, 146-149
Greek .... iii, iv, 3-14, 16-19, 22-24, 26-35, 38-40, 43, 44, 47, 50,
               52-54, 57, 58, 64, 65, 68-73, 76, 77, 79, 80, 87, 89-92, 94-
               97, 99, 102-109, 116, 118, 120, 122-132, 138, 140, 142,
               146-149, 152, 159, 160, 167
Greek Helps 27
Greek MSS 4, 16, 39, 40, 90, 131
Greek Or Aramaic NT? 6
Green 103, 105
HADES 53, 131
heaven 16, 48, 51, 53, 59, 63, 68, 81, 86, 87, 90, 113, 114, 138,
               142
Hebrew .... iii, iv, 11-14, 24, 27, 30, 31, 38-40, 43, 44, 47, 48, 50,
               52-54, 56, 57, 64, 65, 75, 79, 89, 91, 92, 95, 103-109,
               118, 120, 122, 124-127, 129, 131-134, 138, 140-143, 146-
               149, 159, 160, 167
Hebrew & Greek Grammar Books 148
Hebrew lexicon 133, 140, 147
Hebrew Reference Books 142, 147
Hebrew, Aramaic, or Greek Words 64, 109, 120
Hebrews 13, 41, 55, 75, 76, 94, 141
Hebrews 1:8 41
Hebrews 1:8--Christ Is Called God 41
Hell 51-53, 63, 73, 81, 83, 131, 161
Henry 136, 146
heresies 5, 15, 25, 42
Herman Hoskier 7

HEYLEL 109
Hills 40, 129, 130
homosexuality 79
Hort 3-6, 11, 13, 17, 21-24, 27-29, 34, 92, 104, 167
Hoskier 7
How To Get On Our Website 151
How to Pay On-Line 153
Hunt 51, 52
imperfect 30, 47, 57, 91
Independent Baptist Churches 37
Index of Words and Phrases . . . . iv, 169
Inerrancy 46, 47, 125
inerrant 24, 47, 57, 119, 120
inspiration 10, 11, 43, 44, 119, 143
inspired of God 132
Inspired Words 10, 11, 24, 119, 124
Interlinear Greek N.T. 10
Interlinear TR 18
Intermediate Grammar 147, 148
International Baptist College and Seminary 44
Introductory Considerations . . . . iv, 1
Ireland 21
ISBN #1-56848-074-1 i
itself 24-26, 37, 40, 83, 85, 91, 98
Japanese 47, 116
Japanese Bible 116
Jay Green 103
Jay P. Green 105
Jeremiah 47, 56, 127, 138, 144
Jeremiah 34:16 47
Jeremy 127
Jesus Christ's "Prepared Body" 55
John 1:12 . . . . 55, 96
John 3:16 . . . . 38, 59, 63
John 5:7-8 40
John the Baptist 38, 86, 87
Jones 11, 43, 44, 108, 109, 115, 125
Joshua 128
Judgment Of The Nations 161
Judgment seat of Christ 161
kill 73, 133, 134, 136, 137
Kingdom of God 42, 55, 60

Kittel 160
KJB 3-5, 7, 8, 10-14, 27-31, 34, 40, 44, 47, 48, 52-54, 57, 65,
70, 77, 78, 91-96, 98, 99, 103-108, 116, 120-132, 134,
141-143, 145, 146, 159, 165, 167
KJB And The Latin Vulgate 129
KJB In Modern English Possible? 128
KJB Seminar #10 . . . . 27, 125, 126
KJB translators 4, 34, 52, 57, 124, 128, 132, 142, 165
KJV 19, 20, 24, 27, 30, 34, 39, 48, 57, 61, 64, 70, 92, 96, 98,
103-105, 107, 109, 117, 119, 121-123, 129-132, 141, 146,
155, 160
KJV 1611 & Peter Ruckman 132
Kulas 125
Lamb of God 38
Latin 7, 26, 30, 31, 39, 40, 44, 80, 109, 129-131
Latin Vulgate 30, 39, 44, 80, 129-131
law of Moses 62
LB 6, 41, 135
Lectionaries 16, 17
Lesbianism 79
LIMITED ATONEMENT 38
LISTENING TO CURRENT SERVICES LIVE 151
literal Hell fire 51
local church . . . . iii, iv, 126, 155-157, 163
local church matters . . . . iii, iv, 155
LUCIFER 108, 109, 111, 138
LXX 13, 40, 44, 143
Majority Text 10, 19, 30, 32, 33, 43, 147, 149
Maranatha Baptist College 44
Mark 15:2 . . . . 93, 113
Masoretic Text 43, 147
meanings . . . .   iii, iv, 46, 50, 52, 53, 59, 67, 69, 72-75, 78-80, 85-
87, 91, 95, 97-101, 107, 119, 129, 131, 133, 134, 140,
147, 148
Messiah 40, 54, 88, 99, 144
Metzger 15
Michael Sproul 57
Migne 25, 26
minor changes 28
miscellaneous . . . . iii, iv, 145

Miscellaneous Questions iii
Misguided Seminarians 127
modern bible translations 3
Moody Bible Institute 15, 148
Moorman 6, 9, 16, 17, 25, 27, 33, 34, 92, 131, 149
Moorman's Majority Text Book 147
MP-3 Format 27
Mrs. Waite 22, 73
N.T. Canon 50
N.T. Greek Course 17
NA 3-6, 9, 10, 12, 13, 16, 17, 22, 23, 25, 28-30, 32, 33, 37, 41-
        44, 47, 48, 50, 52, 61, 69-72, 74, 76, 80-83, 93, 95, 96,
        99, 100, 102, 104, 105, 107-110, 117, 120, 125, 129, 135-
        138, 140, 142, 144, 147, 148, 156, 159, 161, 165, 167
Nahum 3:16 48
NASB 3, 6, 104, 117
NASV 4, 6, 28, 29, 93, 100, 104, 117, 142
Neologian 9
Nestle 4, 5, 16, 27-29, 33, 104
Nestle-Aland 33
NEV 4
New Testament Greek texts . . . . iii, iv
New Testament word meanings . . . . iii, iv
New Translation For Today? 124
Nicea 38, 39, 51
NIV 3-6, 27-29, 92, 93, 100, 104, 110-115
NKJV 4, 6, 10, 32, 33, 104, 107, 109, 142
NKJV's Greek Text 31
Northland Baptist Bible College 44
NRSV 4, 6, 100
numbers 17, 75, 134, 149
Old Testament Hebrew . . . . iii, iv, 159
Old Testament Word Meanings . . . . iii, iv
omnipresence 41, 42
Omnipresence Of Christ 41
omniscience 41, 42, 90
open to truth 12
Order Blank Pages iv
Orders: 1-800-John 10:9 i
over 3,000 differences 7
Oxford 47, 48, 75, 80, 119, 123, 127, 134
OXFORD & CAMBRIDGE KING JAMES BIBLES 47

Papyrus Fragments 17
passover 70, 71, 93
Pastor D. A. Waite .... i, iii, 47, 151
Pastor Waite 24, 127
Pastors Are Trained In Critical Text 29
Pentecost 48, 50
Perfect 10, 20, 41, 46, 47, 50, 57, 64, 88, 120, 131
Peter 39, 57, 59, 61, 65, 90, 125, 127, 132, 160
Peter Ruckman 57, 65, 125, 127, 132
Ph.D. .... i, iii, 47, 151
Philippians 4:13 .... 76, 77
Pierpont 19, 30, 33
Pilate 93
pleased 114
POD .... ii, 10, 147
Polytheism And The Trinity 61
Pope 4, 81
possible .... ii, iii, 99, 120, 124, 128, 129, 138
Preach the Word 160
print on demand 10, 147
probable 124, 129
process of God's inspiration 10
prophecy............................ iii, iv, 40, 45, 46, 49, 161
Protestant cemetery 4
Proverbs 18:24 142
Psalm 8:4-5 140
Publisher's Data iv
Questions about Miscellaneous Subjects iv
Questions about New Testament Word Meanings iv
Questions about Old Testament Word Meanings iv
Questions about the Chinese Union Version iv
Questions about the King James Bible iv
Questions about the New Testament Greek Texts .... iii, iv
Questions about Theological Problems iv
Questions about Various Bible Versions iv
questions answered 1, 1
Rapture 55, 68, 80-83, 156
regeneration 111
Reina/Valera/Gomez Spanish Bible 165
reject truth 12

Remarriage .... iii, iv, 120, 163
revision 30, 47, 78
Revision Revised 30
Riplinger 65, 132
Robinson 19, 30, 33, 149
Robinson and Pierpont 19, 33
Roman Catholic 23, 39, 69
Roman Catholic Church 39, 69
Roman Catholics 39
Ronald J. Gordon 9
RSV 4, 6, 28, 29, 100, 104, 107, 109, 115, 116, 145
Ruckman 57, 65, 125, 127, 132
RVG 165
safe 105
Saved In Childbearing 54
schools 34, 44, 115, 127
Scofield 42, 68, 127, 132
scribes and Pharisees 113
Scrivener 8, 10, 11, 18, 19, 21, 34, 103
second 200 questions 1
second 200 Questions Answered 1
Second Year Greek 17, 27, 29, 147, 148
seminary 12, 28, 29, 34, 38, 43, 44, 116, 117, 122, 127, 149, 160
Septuagint 13, 39, 40, 44
Sheol 52, 53, 131
Sinai ....,,,,,,.... .... 4, 5, 7, 8, 14, 18, 20, 21, 24, 28, 32, 89, 131
sons of God 55, 64, 77, 96, 141, 146
soul 55, 56, 69, 75, 98, 99
Sound Church Music 155, 156
Spanish .... iii, iv, 12, 14, 23, 47, 129, 165
Spanish Bible .... iii, iv, 14, 129, 165
Speaking In Tongues 48
spirit 15, 16, 43, 45, 48, 49, 56, 58, 59, 61, 69, 84, 88, 90, 141, 142, 155
Spiritual Gifts 45, 48
Spiritual Warfare 63
Sproul 57
Stephanus 11, 23, 57
Stephens 7, 8, 11, 44, 128
Strouse 143
Systematic Theology 122, 152

Table of Contents iv
TBS 160, 165
TELEIOS 46, 50
tenses 86, 91, 108
Textus Receptus 3, 5, 13, 14, 16-20, 24, 28, 29, 31-34, 43, 44,
                        52, 64, 92, 109, 123, 124, 127, 149, 153, 165
Th.D. .... i, iii, 47, 151
That which 21, 46, 50, 68, 85, 113, 116
The 10 Commandments & The N.T. 62
THE BIBLE FOR TODAY PRESS i
The Book of Bible Problems 125
The Cambridge 1769 KJB 123
the Dean Burgon Society .... ii-iv, 10, 15, 16, 34, 46, 167
The Deity Of Christ 40, 41
The Hebrew Old Testament 127, 160
the Spanish Bible .... iii, iv, 129, 165
The Tabernacle 139
The Third 200 Questions Answered 1
The Trinity 16, 59, 61, 62, 115
theological problems .... iii, iv, 37
third series iii
Those So-Called Errors 125
THREE DIFFERENCES 47
tongues 45, 46, 48-50
Tow 26, 68, 125, 144
TR 3-9, 11, 12, 14-20, 23-34, 39-41, 46, 47, 50, 52-54, 56-58,
                61, 64, 65, 67-82, 86, 87, 89-98, 100, 101, 103-113, 116,
                117, 119, 121, 122, 124-126, 128-144, 148, 149, 153,
                                        156, 159, 165, 167
TR Japanese NT 116
Traditional Texts 128
translation errors 47
translators 3, 4, 8, 34, 39, 52, 57, 58, 61, 64, 70, 76, 78, 105,
                    108, 110, 116, 117, 124, 126, 128, 129, 131, 132, 142,
                                                    143, 165
Trinitarian Bible Society 160
Trinity 16, 59-62, 115, 143
Two Creations, Or Only One? 56
two kinds of people 12
Two Natures 42, 43

Two Witnesses In Revelation 161
UBS 4, 5, 28
Uncials 9, 16, 17
United Bible Societies 4, 5, 28, 29, 104
unleavened bread 70
various books .... iii, iv, 7, 145
Various Good Textbooks 146
Vatican 3-5, 7, 8, 14, 18, 20, 21, 24, 26, 28, 32, 131
Vatican and Sinai MSS 4, 131
Vatican manuscript (B) 3
Vatican manuscripts 3
Verbal Plenary Preservation 50
Videos Defending The KJB 126
Vowel Points 138
VPI 44
VPP 44, 50
W&H & Nestle/Aland Greek Texts 27
Waite .... 1, i-iii, 1, 13, 16, 17, 19, 22, 24, 27-29, 47, 73, 92, 126,
                                        127, 145, 146, 148, 149, 151
Wallace 125, 136
Website: www.BibleForToday.org .... i, 151
Westcott 3-6, 11-13, 17, 21-24, 27-29, 34, 41, 92, 104, 167
Westcott and Hort 3-6, 11, 13, 17, 22-24, 27-29, 34, 92, 104,
                                                            167
What Is Dispensationalism? 42
What Is The "Gospel"? 58
What Was Dean Burgon's Beliefs? 167
When the King James Bible Departs from the Majority Text
    10
which 3-6, 8, 10-18, 20-34, 38, 40-46, 48-51, 53-62, 64, 67,
                68, 70-73, 75-78, 80, 81, 85, 86, 88, 90, 91, 94-100, 103-
                111, 113, 115-117, 119, 120, 124-130, 132, 134, 135,
                137-139, 141, 142, 144-148, 155, 156, 159, 163, 165
which is in heaven 113
Who Is "Allah"? 60
whosoever believeth 63
Williams .... ii, 10, 147
worship 5, 62, 79, 80, 139
written by 18, 56, 112
www.BibleForToday.org .... i, 18, 29, 76, 92, 104, 148, 151, 152
Ximenes 7, 23
Young 14, 15, 87, 108, 120, 128, 136, 149

Young's Literal Translation 108, 142
Yvonne Sanborn Waite ii
"Deceit" Or "Error" 85
"Holy Ghost" And "Holy Spirit" 58

About the Author

The author of this book, Dr. D. A. Waite, received a B.A. (Bachelor of Arts) in classical Greek and Latin from the University of Michigan in 1948, a Th.M. (Master of Theology), with high honors, in New Testament Greek Literature and Exegesis from Dallas Theological Seminary in 1952, an M.A. (Master of Arts) in Speech from Southern Methodist University in 1953, a Th.D. (Doctor of Theology), with honors, in Bible Exposition from Dallas Theological Seminary in 1955, and a Ph.D. in Speech from Purdue University in 1961. He holds both New Jersey and Pennsylvania teacher certificates in Greek and Language Arts.

He has been a teacher in the areas of Greek, Hebrew, Bible, Speech, and English for over thirty-five years in ten schools, including one junior high, one senior high, four Bible institutes, two colleges, two universities, and one seminary. He served his country as a Navy Chaplain for five years on active duty; pastored three churches; was Chairman and Director of the Radio and Audio-Film Commission of the American Council of Christian Churches; since 1969, has been Founder, President, and Director of THE BIBLE FOR TODAY; since 1978, has been President of the DEAN BURGON SOCIETY; has produced over 800 other studies, books, audio cassettes, CD's, VCR's, or DVD's on various topics; and is heard on a thirty-minute weekly program, IN DEFENSE OF TRADITIONAL BIBLE TEXTS, on radio, and streaming on the Internet at BibleForToday.org, 24/7/365.

Dr. and Mrs. Waite have been married since 1948; they have four sons, one daughter, and, at present, eight grandchildren, and eleven great-grandchildren. Since October 4, 1998, he has been the Pastor of the Bible For Today Baptist Church in Collingswood, New Jersey.

Order Blank (p. 1)

Name:_____

Address:_____

City & State:_____Zip:_____

*Credit Card #:*_____*Expires:*_____

Latest Books

[ ] Send *The Third 200 Questions Answered* By Dr. D. A. Waite (200 pp. perfect bound ($15.00 + $7.00 S&H)

[ ] Send *The Second 200 Questions Answered* By Dr. D. A. Waite (176 pp. perfect bound ($15.00 + $7.00 S&H)

[ ] Send *The First 200 Questions Answered By Dr. D. A. Waite* (178 pp. perfect bound ($15.00 + $7.00 S&H)

[ ] Send *A Critical Answer to James Price's King James Only-ism* By Pastor D. A. Waite, 184pp, perfect bound ($11+$7 S&H)

[ ] Send *The KJB's Superior Hebrew & Greek Words* by Pastor D. A. Waite, 104 pp., perfect bound ($10+$7 S&H)

[ ] Send *Soulwinning's Versions-Perversions* by Pastor D. A. Waite, booklet, 28 pp. ($6+$5 S&H) fully indexed

[ ] Send *2 Timothy--Preaching Verse by Verse*, by Pastor D. A. Waite, 250 pages, perfect bound ($11+$7 S&H) fully indexed.

[ ] Send *A Critical Answer to God's Word Preserved* by Pastor D. A. Waite, 192 pp. perfect bound ($11.00+$7.00 S&H)

The Most Recently Published Books

[ ] Send *A WARNING!! On Gail Riplinger's KJB & Multiple Inspiration HERESY*, 133 pp. by Pastor DAW ($12+$7 S&H)

[ ] Send *Who Is Gail Riplinger?* 146 pp. by Aleithia O'Brien ($12.00 + $7.00)

[ ] *The Messianic Claims Of Gail A. Riplinger*, By Dr. Phil Stringer, 108 pp., perfect bound ($12.00 + $7.00 S&H)

[ ] Send *8,000 Differences Between Textus Receptus & Critical Text* by Dr. J. A. Moorman, 544 pp., hrd. back ($20+$7 S&H)

Send or Call Orders to:
THE BIBLE FOR TODAY
900 Park Ave., Collingswood, NJ 08108
Phone: 856-854-4452; FAX:--2464; Orders: 1-800 JOHN 10:9
E-Mail Orders: BFT@BibleForToday.org; Credit Cards OK

Order Blank (p. 2)

Name:_____

Address:_____

City & State:_____Zip:_____

Credit Card #:_____Expires:_____

[ ] *Early Manuscripts, Church Fathers, & the Authorized Version* by Dr. Jack Moorman, $20+$7 S&H. Hardback

[ ] Send *The LIE That Changed the Modern World* by Dr. H. D. Williams ($16+$7 S&H) Hardback book

[ ] Send *With Tears in My Heart* by Gertrude G. Sanborn. Hardback 414 pp. ($25+$7 S&H) 400 Christian Poems

Preaching Verse by Verse Books

[ ] Send *2 Timothy--Preaching Verse by Verse*, by Pastor D. A. Waite, 250 pages, hardback ($11+$7 S&H) fully indexed.

[ ] Send *1 Timothy--Preaching Verse by Verse*, by Pastor D. A.Waite, 288 pages, hardback ($14+$7 S&H) fully indexed.

More Preaching Verse by Verse Books

[ ] Send *Romans--Preaching Verse by Verse* by Pastor D. A. Waite 736 pp. Hardback ($25+$7 S&H) fully indexed

[ ] Send *Colossians & Philemon--Preaching Verse by Verse* by Pastor D. A. Waite ($12+$7 S&H) hardback, 240 pages

[ ] Send *Philippians--Preaching Verse by Verse* by Pastor D. A. Waite ($10+$7 S&H) hardback, 176 pages

[ ] Send *Ephesians--Preaching Verse by Verse* by Pastor D. A. Waite ($12+$7 S&H) hardback, 224 pages

[ ] Send *Galatians--Preaching Verse By Verse* by Pastor D. A. Waite ($13+$7 S&H) hardback, 216 pages

[ ] Send *First Peter--Preaching Verse By Verse* by Pastor D. A. Waite ($10+$7 S&H) hardback, 176 pages

Books on Bible Texts & Translations

[ ] Send *Defending the King James Bible* by DAW ($12+$7 S&H) A hardback book, indexed with study questions

Send or Call Orders to:
THE BIBLE FOR TODAY
900 Park Ave., Collingswood, NJ 08108
Phone: 856-854-4452; FAX:--2464; Orders: 1-800 JOHN 10:9
E-Mail Orders: BFT@BibleForToday.org; Credit Cards OK

Order Blank (p. 3)

Name:_____

Address:_____

City & State:_____Zip:_____

Credit Card #:_____Expires:_____

[ ] Send *BJU's Errors on Bible Preservation* by Dr. D. A. Waite, 110 pages, paperback ($8+$7 S&H) fully indexed

[ ] Send *Fundamentalist Deception on Bible Preservation* by Dr.Waite, ($8+$4 S&H), paperback, fully indexed

[ ] Send *Fundamentalist MIS-INFORMATION on Bible Versions* by Dr. Waite ($7+$5 S&H) perfect bound, 136 pages

[ ] Send *Fundamentalist Distortions on Bible Versions* by Dr.Waite ($7+$4 S&H) A perfect bound book, 80 pages

[ ] Send *Fuzzy Facts From Fundamentalists* by Dr. D. A. Waite ($8.00 + $7.00 S&H)

More Books on Bible Texts & Translations

[ ] Send *Foes of the King James Bible Refuted* by DAW ($9 +$7 S&H) A perfect bound book, 164 pages in length

[ ] Send *Central Seminary Refuted on Bible Versions* by Dr. Waite ($10+$7 S&H) A perfect bound book, 184 pages

[ ] Send *The Case for the King James Bible* by DAW ($8 +$5 S&H) A perfect bound book, 112 pages in length

[ ] Send *Theological Heresies of Westcott and Hort* by Dr. D. A. Waite, ($8+$5 S&H) A printed booklet

[ ] Send *Westcott's Denial of Resurrection*, Dr. Waite ($8+$5)

[ ] Send *Four Reasons for Defending KJB* by DAW ($4+$3)

More Books on Texts & Translations

[ ] Send *Holes in the Holman Christian Standard Bible* by Dr. Waite ($6+$4 S&H) A printed booklet, 40 pages

[ ] Send *Contemporary Eng. Version Exposed*, DAW ($6+$4)

[ ] Send *NIV Inclusive Language Exposed* by DAW ($7+$5)

Send or Call Orders to:
THE BIBLE FOR TODAY
900 Park Ave., Collingswood, NJ 08108
Phone: 856-854-4452; FAX:--2464; Orders: 1-800 JOHN 10:9
E-Mail Orders: BFT@BibleForToday.org; Credit Cards OK

Order Blank (p. 5)

Name:_____

Address:_____

City & State:_____Zip:_____

Credit Card #:_____Expires:_____

[ ] Send *The Last 12 verses of Mark* by Dean Burgon ($15+$7 S&H) A hardback book 400 pages

[ ] Send *The Traditional Text* hardback by Burgon ($15+$5 S&H) A hardback book, 384 pages in length

[ ] Send *Causes of Corruption* by Burgon ($16+$5 S&H) A hardback book, 360 pages in length

More Books By or About Dean Burgon

[ ] Send *Inspiration and Interpretation*, Dean Burgon ($25+$7 S&H) A hardback book, 610 pages in length

[ ] Send *Burgon's Warnings on Revision* by DAW ($7+$5 S&H) A perfect bound book, 120 pages in length

[ ] Send *Westcott & Hort's Greek Text & Theory Refuted by Burgon's Revision Revised--Summarized* by Dr. D. A. Waite ($7.00+$5 S&H), 120 pages, perfect bound

[ ] Send *Dean Burgon's Confidence in KJB* by DAW ($5+$4)

[ ] Send *Vindicating Mark 16:9-20* by Dr. Waite ($5+$4S&H)

[ ] Send *Summary of Traditional Text* by Dr. Waite ($5 +$4)

[ ] Send *Summary of Causes of Corruption*, DAW ($5+$4)

[ ] Send *Summary of Inspiration* by Dr. Waite ($5+$4 S&H)

More Books by Dr. D. A. Waite

[ ] Send *Making Marriage Melodious* by Pastor D. A. Waite ($7+$5 S&H), perfect bound, 112 pages

Books by D. A. Waite, Jr.

[ ] Send *Readability of A.V. (KJB)* by D. A. Waite, Jr. ($7+$4)

[ ] Send *4,114 Definitions from the Defined King James Bible* by D. A. Waite, Jr. ($7.00+$5.00 S&H)

Send or Call Orders to:
THE BIBLE FOR TODAY
900 Park Ave., Collingswood, NJ 08108
Phone: 856-854-4452; FAX:--2464; Orders: 1-800 JOHN 10:9
E-Mail Orders: BFT@BibleForToday.org; Credit Cards OK

Order Blank (p. 6)

Name:_____

Address:_____

City & State:_____Zip:_____

Credit Card #:_____Expires:_____
[ ] Send *The Doctored New Testament* by D. A. Waite, Jr.
   ($25+$7.00 S&H) Greek MSS differences shown, hardback
[ ] Send *Defined King James Bible* lg. prt. leather ($40+$10)
[ ] Send *Defined King James Bible* med. leather $35+$8.50)

Miscellaneous Authors

[ ] Send *Wycliffe Controversies* by Dr. H. D. Williams,
   perfect bound, 311 pages @ $20.00 + $7.00 S&H
[ ] Send *The Pure Words of God* by Dr. H. D. Williams,
   perfect bound ($15.00 + $7.00 S&H)
[ ] Send *Hearing the Voice of God* by Dr. H. D. Williams,
   perfect bound ($18.00 + $7.00 S&H)
[ ] Send *The Attack on the Canon of Scripture* by Dr. H. D.
   Williams, perfect bound ($15.00 + $7.00 S&H)
[ ] Send *Word-For-Word Translating of The Received Texts* by
   Dr. H. D. Williams, 288 pages, paperback ($10+$7 S&H).
[ ] Send *Guide to Textual Criticism* by Edward Miller
   ($11+$7 S&H) a hardback book
[ ] Send *Scrivener's Greek New Testament Underlying the
   King James Bible*, hardback, ($14 + $7 S&H)
[ ] Send *Scrivener's Annotated Greek New Testament*, by Dr.
   Frederick Scrivener: Hardback--($35+$7 S&H);
   Genuine Leather--($45+$7 S&H)
[ ] Send *Why Not the King James Bible?--An Answer to James
   White's KJVO Book* by Dr. K. D. DiVietro, $10+$7 S&H
[ ] Send Brochure #1: "Over *1000 Titles Defending the
KJB/TR*" No Charge

Send or Call Orders to:
THE BIBLE FOR TODAY
900 Park Ave., Collingswood, NJ 08108
Phone: 856-854-4452; FAX:--2464; Orders: 1-800 JOHN 10:9

www.ingramcontent.com/pod-product-compliance
Lightning Source LLC
Chambersburg PA
CBHW071432090426
42737CB00011B/1637